MW01267979

The Life of David Livingstone

MISSIONARY ANNALS.

(A SERIES

THE LIFE OF

DAVID LIVINGSTONE.

BY

MRS. J. H WORCESTER, JR.

FLEMING H. REVELL COMPANY,

CHICAGO.   NEW YORK   TORONTO.

Publishers Evangelical Literature.

CONTENTS.

CHAPTER I.

DAVID LIVINGSTONE was born in Blantyre, Scotland, March 19th, 1813. His father and mother were people of lowly station, and he was reared in poverty. The story of his origin is briefly told in the simple inscription which he caused to be placed upon the monument to his parents, at a time when the highest in the land were showering compliments upon him.

> "To show the resting place of
> NEIL LIVINGSTONE,
> and AGNES HUNTER, his wife,
> and to express the thankfulness to God
> of their children,
> John, David, Janet, Charles and Agnes,
> for poor and pious parents."

An inscription whose last deliberately chosen "and" he distinctly refused to exchange for a "but."

Both of Livingstone's parents were earnestly devout, the mother an active, sunny, loving woman, and the father, as David himself bore witness, of the high type of character portrayed in the *Cotter's Saturday Night*. Neil Livingstone was a strict teetotaler, a Sunday-school teacher, an ardent member of a missionary society, and a promoter of prayer-meetings, at a time when none of these things had ceased to be regarded as badges of fanaticism. While travelling through the adjoining parishes in his vocation of tea-merchant he often acted as colporteur, distributing tracts, and showing in various ways that his was the true missionary spirit.

The home in which David Livingstone grew up, although enriched by little beyond the bare necessaries of life, was brightened and made happy by industry, cheerfulness, love for one another, and faith in God.

Of David's early boyhood we know little, except that he was a favorite at home, always contributing to the happiness of the family, and that he seems to have been from his earliest childhood of a calm, self-reliant nature. It was his father's habit to lock the outer door at dusk, at which time all the children were expected to be in the house. One evening David found the door barred when he reached home. He made no outcry or disturbance, but sat down contentedly to pass the night on the doorstep. There, on looking out, his mother found him. It was an early application of the rule which did him such service later in life, to make the best of the least pleasant situations. As a proof of his perseverance, we read that at the age of nine he received a New Testament from his Sabbath-school teacher for repeating the 119th Psalm on two successive evenings, with only five errors.

His parents were so poor that at the age of ten he was set to work in a factory. With a part of his first week's wages he purchased a Latin grammar. Though working from six in the morning until eight at night, with intervals only for breakfast and dinner, he attended an evening class from eight to ten, and pursued his studies with much enthusiasm. Often, indeed, he continued his labors after reaching home, until midnight or later, unless his mother interfered. At the age of sixteen he was thus familiar with Virgil and Horace, and many of the classical authors. In his reading he devoured everything but novels, placing his book on a portion of the spinning-jenny, so that he could catch sentence after sentence as he passed at his work. The utmost interval that Livingstone could have had for reading at one time was less than a minute, but, as he afterwards writes:

"I thus kept up a pretty constant study, undisturbed by the roar of the machinery. To this part of my education I owe my power of completely abstracting my mind from surrounding noise, so as to read and write with perfect comfort amidst the play of children or the dancing and songs of savages."

Like other boys he was fond of play and fun, but with a growing thirst for knowledge. Books of travel and of science were his especial delight, and when a rare half-holiday came round he was usually to be found at the quarries collecting geological specimens, or by the hedge-rows gathering herbs and flowers. He early formed the opinion that a good herbalist has in his hands the panacea for all bodily diseases.

David was not very fond of religious reading, and he tells us, with that quiet humor which never deserted him, that his last flogging was received for refusing to read Wilberforce's *Practical Christianity*. This dislike continued for years, until he lighted upon Dick's *Philosophy of Religion* and *Philosophy of a Future State*, which he found, to his delight, enforced his own conviction that religion and science were friendly to each other.

It was while reading the last-named book that he became convinced that it was his duty and highest privilege to accept of Christ's salvation for himself. This was in his twentieth year. He had had many earnest thoughts about religion for years, but only now did the great spiritual change occur.

"This change," he says, "was like what may be supposed

would take place were it possible to cure a case of ' color-
blindness.' The fullness with which the pardon of all our
guilt is offered in God's book drew forth feelings of affectionate love to Him who bought us with His blood, which
in some small measure has influenced my conduct ever
since."

"There can be no doubt that Livingstone's heart was
very thoroughly penetrated by the new life that now flowed
into it. He did not merely apprehend the truth. The truth
took hold of him."

Although at first he had no thought of becoming a missionary himself, he made a resolution that, as the salvation
of men ought to be the chief aim of every Christian, he
would give to the cause of missions all that he could earn
beyond what was required for his subsistence. It was about
a year later that, after reading Dr. Gutzlaff's "Appeal" on
behalf of China, he resolved to give himself to the work in that
country. "The claims of so many millions of his fellow-
creatures, and the complaint of the want of qualified men to
undertake the task" were, as he informs us, the motives
which led him to this high resolve; henceforth his "efforts
were constantly directed towards that object without any
fluctuation." In addition to the necessary theological training, he determined also to acquire that needed by a physician. Though it was never his lot to exercise the healing art
in China, his medical knowledge was of the highest use in
Africa, and it developed wonderfully his strong scientific
turn.

While pursuing his medical studies in Glasgow it involved
much self-denial on Livingstone's part to make the wages
earned during the summer suffice for all his needs, and many
less determined would have ended the struggle there and

then. But Livingstone was made of different stuff, as these words of his, written years later, show:

"Were I to begin life over again, I should like to pass through the same hardy training. I never received a farthing from any one, and I should have accomplished my project of going to China as a medical missionary by my own efforts, had not some friends advised my joining the London Missionary Society, on account of its unsectarian character. It 'sends neither Episcopacy, nor Presbyterianism, nor Independency, but the gospel of Christ, to the heathen.' This exactly agreed with my ideas of what a missionary society ought to do; but it was not without a pang that I offered myself, for it was not agreeable to one accustomed to work his own way to become in a measure dependent on others."

Livingstone had already connected himself with the Independent, or Congregational Church. He had very strong views of the need of a deep, spiritual change as the only true basis of Christian life and character, and his preference for this branch of the church universal arose mainly from the feeling that the Presbyterian Churches of Scotland, and the Established Church in particular, were at this time too lax in their communion. But never was a man more free from sectarianism than he.

It was in 1838 that Livingstone applied to the London Missionary Society, offering his services as a missionary, and his application was provisionally accepted. In September of that year he was summoned to London to meet the directors, and after passing two examinations he was sent to study with Rev. Richard Cecil, to whom most missionary students were sent for a three months' probation. One part of his duties was to prepare sermons, which, when corrected, were committed to memory and repeated to village congregations.

Once Livingstone was sent for to preach in a neighboring pulpit, the pastor having been taken suddenly ill. He took his text, read it slowly, and then — all was a blank. Not a word could he remember of his carefully prepared sermon. Saying abruptly, " Friends, I have forgotten all I had to say," he hurried out of the pulpit and left the chapel. Owing to this failure and to general lack of fluency in prayer, an unfavorable report was sent in when the three months had elapsed ; but·some one urged that he should have a still further probation, and a few months later he was accepted.

It was a disappointment to him that he could not carry out his original intention of preaching the gospel in China, but the opium war had closed that country to the English, and while it continued no new appointments could be made. It was in these circumstances that he met Robert Moffat, who, after twenty-three years of labor in South Africa, was thrilling England with the story of his work and adventures there. He fired the soul of his young countryman with a desire to explore and evangelize that " dark continent " with which both their names are now identified.

Under Moffat's influence, then, Livingstone determined to go at once to Africa, and in this decision the directors concurred. Henceforth Africa was to be his sphere.

It was felt that a medical diploma would be of service, and Livingstone received this in November, 1840. A single night was all he could spend with his family, and they had so much to talk about that David proposed they should sit up all night, though to this his mother would not listen. " I remember my father and him," writes his sister, " talking over the prospects of Christian missions. They agreed that the time would come when rich men and great men would think it an honor to support whole stations of missionaries, instead of spending their money on hounds and horses. On the morning of 17th November we got up at five o'clock. My mother made coffee. David read the 121st and 135th Psalms, and prayed. My father and he walked to Glasgow to catch the Liverpool steamer." On the Broomielaw father and son looked on each other's faces for the last time on earth. The one walked slowly back to Blantyre, his heart full of mingling emotions of sorrow and joy. The face of the **other** was now set in earnest towards the "dark continent."

CHAPTER II.

KURUMAN TO KOLOBENG.

ON the 20th of November, 1840, Livingstone was ordained a missionary, and on December 8th he embarked for Algoa Bay. During the voyage his chief friend was the captain of the ship, who was very obliging, giving him all the information respecting the use of the quadrant in his power, and frequently sitting up till midnight for the purpose of taking lunar observations with him. Thus another qualification was acquired for Livingstone's peculiar life-work. His first letter to the directors of the London Missionary Society displayed his characteristic honesty, saying that he had spent most of his time at sea in the study of theology, and that he was deeply grieved to say that he knew of no spiritual good having been done in the case of any one on board the ship.

After reaching Algoa Bay, Livingstone proceeded at once to Kuruman, in the Bechuana country, where he arrived in July, 1841. This was the most northerly station of the society in South Africa, being 700 miles north of Cape Town, and was the usual residence of Mr. Moffat, who was still absent in England. Livingstone's instructions were to remain there until Mr. Moffat's return, and turn his attention to the formation of a new station farther north. While awaiting more specific instructions he began to entertain the idea of going to Abyssinia. A Christian missionary was evidently needed there, for the country had none, but if he should go he felt that probably he should never return. We hear no more of the project, but writing of this to a friend, he uses these almost prophetic words: "Whatever way my life may be spent as best to promote the glory of our gracious God, I feel anxious to do it. . . . *My life may be spent as profitably as a pioneer as in any other way.*"

After a short time spent in Kuruman, ne went to a spot where he secluded himself from all European society for about six months, in order to obtain a knowledge of the native tongue. Livingstone gained by this ordeal an insight into the habits, ways of thinking, laws and language of the Bakwains, which proved of incalculable advantage in his intercourse with them ever after.

Livingstone's life in Africa resolves itself into four distinct periods. First, that of ordinary mission work, upon which he was now entering; second, that of the first great journey under the auspices of the London Missionary Society; third, that of the exploration of the Zambesi at the head of a gov ernment expedition; fourth, the journeys under the general direction of the Royal Geographical Society.

Soon after his arrival at Kuruman, Livingstone became convinced that there was not enough population at that point to justify a concentration of missionary labor there, and that efforts should be made speedily to reach the teeming multitudes in the interior. He also believed in making the utmost possible use of native agency in order to cultivate so wide a field. A journey of 700 miles, taken with a brother missionary, tended strongly to confirm these views, and led to the selection of a station 250 miles north of Kuruman, which was not, however, entered upon until 1843.

Before Livingstone had been a year in the country his power over the Africans was manifest. His fearless manner, his genial address, and his genuine kindness of heart, united to form a spell which rarely failed. His medical knowledge helped him greatly; but for permanent influence all would have been in vain, had he not uniformly observed the rules of good manners, justice, and good feeling.

Just a year after his arrival he writes to his father: "The work of God goes on here notwithstanding all our infirmities. Souls are gathered in continually, and sometimes from among those you would never have expected to see turning to the Lord. Twenty-four were added to the church last month, and there are several inquirers."

Already Livingstone could preach in one dialect, and was learning another. His heart was full of the missionary spirit, but the activity of his mind enabled him at the same time to give attention to other matters. He had the rare faculty of directing his mind at the full stretch of its power to one great object, and yet, apparently without effort, giving minute attention to minor matters, all bearing, however, on the same great end. In his missionary journeys he made the acquaintance of the two great foes of the explorer in Africa, fever and the venomous tsetse fly. Fever he considered the greatest barrier to the evangelization of the country, while the tsetse fly was the greatest enemy of beasts of burden, frequently destroying every ox in a team. Its sting, however, was comparatively harmless to men, or exploration would have been entirely out of the question.

In 1843 Livingstone visited Sechele, chief of the Bakwains, afterward one of his greatest friends. Sechele had been enraged at him for not visiting him when he had been in the vicinity the year before, and had threatened him with mischief. But when the missionary arrived his only child was ill, and also the child of one of his principal men. Under Livingstone's treatment both were restored to health, and Sechele was thoroughly conciliated.

It was not until his return to Kuruman from this journey, in June, 1843, that Livingstone at last found, to his great satisfaction, a letter from the directors authorizing the formation of a settlement in the regions beyond. He lost no time in opening a station at Mabotsa, a beautiful valley surrounded by mountains.

There was one drawback to the new locality; it was infested with lions. Here it was that the encounter with the lion occurred which came so near ending Livingstone's career. With characteristic modesty, writing to his father of this serious encounter, he says, after expressing his gratitude for God's mercy in sparing his life, "Do not mention this to any one. I do not like to be talked about." Yielding, however, to the solicitations of friends, Livingstone goes somewhat into details in his *Missionary Travels*.

He says that the people were much troubled by lions, which attacked their cattle even in open day. Knowing that if one in a troop of lions is killed the rest leave that part of the country, he encouraged the natives to endeavor to destroy one of the marauders. He succeeded in shooting a lion himself, but before he could load again the beast had sprung upon him. "The lion caught me by the shoulder and we both came to the ground together. Growling horribly, he shook me as a terrier dog does a rat. The shock produced a stupor similar to that which seems to be felt by a mouse after the first gripe of the cat. . . . It was like what patients partially under the influence of chloroform describe; they see the operation, but do not feel the knife. This placidity is probably produced in all animals killed by the carnivora, and if so, is a merciful provision of the Creator for lessening the pain of death." Mebalwe, one of the natives, endeavored to shoot the lion, which immediately left Livingstone to attack him, biting him in the thigh. Another man now attempted to spear the savage beast, which turned from Mebalwe to the new foe, when the bullets he had received took effect and he fell dead. Besides crunching the bones into splinters, eleven of his teeth had penetrated the upper part of Livingstone's left arm, which, being imperfectly set, was maimed for life.

It is generally known that it was by the false joint in the broken arm that Livingstone's body was identified when brought back to England by his faithful followers; but it is not as well known that Mebalwe, who saved his life, was one of the native teachers that he himself had trained, and that it was a Christian lady in Scotland who contributed the money for this catechist's support. Little did she think that her gift of twelve pounds would indirectly be the means of preserving the life of Africa's greatest benefactor for the wonderful work of the next thirty years! Mebalwe was still alive in 1881, a useful man, an able preacher, and one who had done much to bring his people to Christ.

The next year saw Livingstone established in the new stone house of which he was both architect and builder, and happy in the companionship of his young bride, Mary Moffat, the eldest daughter of the missionary through whose influence he had come to Africa. From 1840 to 1845 he was employed in preparatory labors, and associated with other missionaries both at Kuruman and Mabotsa; but it is melancholy to read that from this first home and station of his own he was driven by the jealousy of a colleague, who was vexed at the attention attracted in England by Livingstone's missionary letters. But Dr. Livingstone's noble spirit rose to the occasion. Although feeling keenly the injustice done him, rather than have any scandal before the heathen he would begin anew the toil of house and school building, and gathering the people about him.

On leaving Mabotsa Livingstone transferred his services to the Bakwains, whose chief, Sechele, and his people, had expressed a strong desire to have a missionary reside among them. The new station of Chonuane, forty miles from Mabotsa, was chosen, but their residence here was of short duration. The want of rain was fatal to agriculture, and almost equally so to the mission. Dr. Livingstone had showed the chief that the only feasible way of watering the gardens was to select a site near some never-failing river, make a canal, and irrigate the adjacent lands. His wonderful influence over the tribe is apparent in the fact that the very morning after he had told them of his intention to move to Kolobeng, they were all preparing to go with him. There, besides making a canal, building huts, and making gardens, they soon set about the erection of a school-house. This work, employing about 200 of his people, was undertaken by Sechele. "I desire," he said, "to build a house for God, the defender of my town, and that you be at no expense for it whatever." At Kolobeng Livingstone built his third house, where for the next five years he had his last home on earth.

In his first book what he calls "a sketch of African house-keeping," is given as follows:

"The entire absence of shops obliged us to make everything we needed from the raw materials. If you want bricks to build a house you must proceed to the field, cut down a tree, and saw it into planks to make the brick-moulds. The people cannot assist you much; for, though willing to labor for wages, the Bakwains have a curious inability to make things square. As with all Bechuanas, their own dwellings are round. I erected three large houses at different times,

2

and every brick and stick had to be put square by my own hand. A house of decent dimensions, costing an immense amount of manual labor, is necessary to secure the respect of the natives.

"Bread is often baked in an extempore oven, constructed by scooping out a large hole in an ant-hill, and using a slab of stone for a door. Another plan is to make a good fire on the ground, and when it is thoroughly heated to place the dough in a short-handled frying-pan, or simply on the hot ashes. A metal pot is then put over it, and a small fire is kindled on the top.

"We made our own candles, and soap was procured from the ashes of the plant salsola, or else from wood ashes, which in Africa contain so little alkaline matter that the boiling of successive lyes has to be continued for a month or six weeks before the fat is saponified.

"We rose early, because, however hot the day, the evening, night and morning at Kolobeng were deliciously refreshing. After family worship and breakfast between six and seven, we kept school, men, women, and children being all invited. This lasted till eleven o'clock. The missionary's wife then betook herself to her domestic affairs, and the missionary engaged in some manual labor, as that of a smith, carpenter or gardener. Dinner and an hour's rest succeeded, when the wife attended her infant school, which the young liked amazingly and generally mustered a hundred strong; or she varied it with sewing-classes for the girls, which was equally well relished. After sunset the husband went into the town to converse, either on general subjects or on religion. We had a public service on three nights of the week, and on another instruction on secular subjects aided by pictures and specimens. In addition to these duties we proscribed for the sick, and furnished food to the poor. The smallest acts of friendship, even an obliging word and civil look, are, as St. Xavier thought, no despicable part of the missionary's armor. Nor ought the good opinion of the most abject to be neglected when politeness may secure it. Their good word in the aggregate forms a reputation which procures favor for the gospel. Show kindness to the reckless opponents of Christianity on the bed of sickness, and they can never become your personal enemies. Here, if anywhere, love begets love."

Again he writes: "A native smith taught me to weld iron, and having acquired some further information in this art as well as in carpentering and gardening from Mr. Moffat, I was becoming handy at most mechanical employments in addition to medicine and preaching. My wife could make candles, soap, and clothes; and thus we had nearly attained to the indispensable accomplishments of a missionary family in Central Africa — the husband to be a jack-of-all trades without doors, and the wife a maid-of-all-work within."

We can well realize that with the utmost frugality it was sometimes difficult to "make both ends meet," when we learn that until 1853 all the extra expenses of travelling, though for the wider diffusion of the gospel, were defrayed from his own meagre salary of £100 per annum. This salary would have enabled a missionary to live with tolerable comfort in the interior of South Africa provided he had a garden producing corn and vegetables, but otherwise the allowance was barely sufficient for the poorest fare and plainest apparel. Now the cost of missionary travels, the liberal gifts which *had* to be made to chiefs, the wants of an increasing family, (he had now four children, three boys and a girl,) added to the ordinary expenses of living, rendered the closest

economy necessary, and of course they had many privations
and trials. Yet theirs was truly a happy life notwithstanding. In reviewing this part of his career in Africa, Livingstone only regrets that he did not devote more time to play-
ing with his children; but our only wonder is that he could
have found time to accomplish all that he did. It is not
strange that, as he says, he was generally so exhausted by
the mental and manual labor of the day, that in the evening
there was no·fun left in him.

CHAPTER III.

CONVERSION OF SECHELE.

THE first fruit of Livingstone's missionary labor in this region was the conversion of Sechele, that chief of whom we have already heard. The little sketch of his life which follows is taken verbatim from Livingstone's *Missionary Travels*, though with some omissions:

"I was from the first struck by his intelligence, and by the especial manner in which we felt drawn to each other. This remarkable man has not only embraced Christianity, but expounds its doctrines to his people. . . . On the first occasion in which I ever attempted to hold a public religious service, Sechele remarked that it was the custom of his nation to put questions when any new subject was brought before them. He then inquired if my forefathers knew of a future judgment. I replied in the affirmative, and began to describe the scene of the great white throne, and Him who shall sit on it, from whose face the heaven and earth shall flee away. 'You startle me,' he replied; 'these words make all my bones to shake; I have no more strength in me; but my forefathers were living at the same time yours were, and how is it that they did not send them word about these terrible things sooner? They all passed away into darkness without knowing whither they were going.' . . .

"As soon as he had an opportunity of learning, he set himself to read with such close application that, from being comparatively thin, the effect of being addicted to the chase, he became corpulent from want of exercise. He acquired the alphabet on the first day of my residence at Chonuane, and I never went into the town but I was pressed to hear him read some chapters of the Bible. Isaiah was a great favorite with him, and he was wont to exclaim, 'He was a fine man, that Isaiah; he knew how to speak.'

"He seconded my anxiety that his subjects should become converts to Christianity, and said, 'Do you imagine these people will ever believe by your merely talking to them? I can make them do nothing except by threatening them; and if you like, I shall call my head men, and with our whips of rhinoceros-hide we will soon make them all believe together.' The idea of using persuasion to subjects, whose opinion he would not have condescended to ask on any other matter, was especially surprising to him. He considered that they ought to be happy to embrace Christianity at his command.

"He felt the difficulties of his situation, and often said, 'Oh, I wish you had come to this country before I was entangled in the meshes of our customs!' In fact, he could not get rid of his superfluous wives without appearing to be ungrateful to their parents, who had done so much for him in his adversity.

"In the hope of inducing others to accept his new faith, he asked me to have family worship in his own house. This I did, and by and by I was surprised to hear how well he conducted the prayer in his own simple and beautiful style, for he was a thorough master of his language. At this time we were suffering from the effects of a drought, which was ascribed by the natives to Christianity, and none except his family, whom he ordered to attend, came near his meeting. 'In former times,' said he, 'when a chief was fond of hunting, all his people got dogs and became fond of hunting too. If he was fond of dancing or music, all showed a liking to these amusements too. If the chief loved beer, they all rejoiced in strong drink. But in this case it is different. I love the Word of God, and not one of my brethren will join me.'

"When he at last — in 1848 — applied for baptism, I asked him how, being acquainted with the Bible, he thought he ought to act. He went home and gave each of his supernumerary wives new clothing, together with all the goods they had been accustomed to keep in their huts for him. He then sent them to their parents with an intimation that he had no fault to find with them, but that he wished to follow the will of God. When he and his children were baptized, great numbers came to see the ceremony. Some thought from a stupid story which had been circulated by the enemies to Christianity in the South, that the converts would be made to drink an infusion of ' dead men's brains,' and were astonished to find that only water was used. Seeing several old men in tears during the service, I afterwards asked them the cause of their weeping. They were crying to see their father, as the Scotch remark of a case of suicide, '*so far left to himself.*' They seemed to think that I had thrown the glamour over him, and that he had become mine. All the friends of the divorced wives now became the opponents of our religion. The attendance at school and church dwindled down to very few besides the family of the chief. They all continued to treat us with respectful kindness ; but to Sechele himself they uttered things which, had they ventured on in former times, would, as he often remarked, have cost them their lives."

Later we learn that Sechele himself had become a missionary to his own people, and had considerable influence over them, though more in material than in religious matters. He was always a warm friend of missions, had a remarkable

knowledge of the Bible, and could preach well. His regard
for the memory of Livingstone was very great, and he read
with earnestness everything that he could find about him.
Notwithstanding that Sechele's efforts were not as successful
as had been hoped, the results show that Livingstone had laid
a good foundation. "That mission," writes Dr. Moffat in
1874, "is the most prosperous, extensive, and influential of
all our missions in the Bechuana country."

In 1881 Sechele was still living, with the one wife whom
he had retained, and though not without some inconsistencies
of life — which Livingstone ascribed to the bad example set
him by some — he still maintained his Christian profession.
His people, being at some miles' distance from Kolobeng, had
now a missionary station of their own supported by a
Hanoverian Society.

CHAPTER IV.

DIFFICULTIES AND DISCOVERIES.

NOT only in these scenes of active missionary labor, but wherever he was, Livingstone was in the habit of preaching to the natives, and talking with them on religious topics, especially the love of Christ, the Fatherhood of God, the resurrection, and the last judgment. Dr. Moffat tells us that his preaching was simple, scriptural, interesting, very direct, and well suited to the capacity of the people.

Livingstone never expected that the work of real Christianity would advance rapidly among the Bakwains, for they were a slow people and took long to move; but it was not his desire to have a large church of nominal adherents. "Nothing" he writes, "will induce me to form an impure church. Fifty added to the church sounds fine at home, but if only five of these are genuine what will it profit in the Great Day? I have felt more than ever lately that the great object of our exertions ought to be conversion." For two years he allowed no celebration of the Lord's Supper, because he did not deem the professing Christians to be living consistent lives. Here was a crowning proof of his hatred of all sham and his love for thorough, finished work. To his father he writes (July 5, 1848): "For a long time I felt much depressed after preaching the unsearchable riches of Christ to apparently insensible hearts; but now I like to dwell on the love of the great Mediator, for it always warms my own heart, and I know that the gospel is the power of God — the great means which He employs for the regeneration of our ruined world."

Again he writes: "We have a difficult, difficult field to cultivate here. All I can say is that I think knowledge is increasing. But for the belief that the Holy Spirit works and will work for us, I should give up in despair. Remember us in your prayers, that we grow not weary in well-doing. It is hard to work for years with pure motives, and all the time be looked on by most of those to whom our lives are devoted, as having some sinister object in view. Disinterested labor — benevolence — is so out of their line of thought that many look upon us as having some ulterior object in view. But He who died for us, and whom we ought to copy, did more for us than we can do for any one else. He endured the contradiction of sinners. May we have grace to follow in His steps!"

One serious obstacle to the rapid spread of the gospel was the continued drought that followed the Bakwains even to Kolobeng. During two years the total amount of rain-fall was not more than ten inches, while there was an abundance of rain all around them. As the tribe had not suffered from successive droughts before the gospel was made known to them, it was natural that they should draw unfavorable inferences.

In his *Missionary Travels*, Livingstone writes: " The belief in the power of *rain making* is one of the most deeply rooted articles of faith in this country. The chief Sechele was himself a noted rain-doctor, and he often assured me that he found it more difficult to give up this superstition than anything else that Christianity required him to abjure. The Bakwains believed that I had bound Sechele with some magic spell, and I received deputations of the old counselors, entreating me to allow him to make only a few showers. ' The corn will die if you refuse, and we shall become scattered. Only let him make rain this once, and we shall all, men, women, and children, come to the school, and sing and pray as long as you please.' . . . The Bakwains still went on treating us with kindness, and I am not aware of ever having had an enemy in the tribe; but as they believed that there must be some connection between the presence of 'God's Word' in their town, and these successive droughts, they looked with no good-will at the church-bell. 'We like you' said the uncle of Sechele, a very influential and sensible person, 'as well as if you had been born among us; you are the only white man we can become familiar with; but we wish you to give up that everlasting preaching and praying; we cannot become familiar with that at all. You see we never get rain, while these tribes who never pray as we do obtain abundance.'"

Sometimes the attendance at the church services was exceedingly small. At one such time, we are told, a bellman of a somewhat peculiar order was employed to collect the people together. "Up he jumped," continues the narrative, "on a sort of platform, and shouted at the top of his voice, 'Knock that woman down over there. Strike her, she is putting on her pot! Do you see that one hiding herself? Give her a good blow. There she is — see! see! Knock her down!' All the women ran to the place of meeting in no time, for each thought herself meant. But, though a most efficient bellman, we did not like to employ him."

During this period of life in Kolobeng, Livingstone's ordinary missionary avocations of preaching, teaching, practicing medicine, and working at all manner of trades, were interrupted by several long journeys of 400 or 500 miles to the north, to visit the country of the Makololo, a large tribe, who, as he was told, were very desirious of having a

missionary. It was becoming evident that Kolobeng must
ere long be abandoned. Already the river was dried up, and
the absence of water, and consequently of food in the gardens, made it necessary for the men to be often at a distance hunting, and for the women to be away collecting
locusts, so that frequently there was hardly any one to come
to church or school. If this station, too, had to be abandoned,
where should Livingstone go next? It had not been his
intention to remain always with the Bakwains, and it was
certainly worth while to see if a suitable locality could not
be found among the Makololo. If the new region were not
suitable for himself, he might at least find openings for native
teachers.

Driven back by fever and other obstacles, it was only in
the third attempt that he succeeded in reaching the village
of the chief of the Makololo, Sebituane. This man was very
friendly to Livingstone, who thought him the best specimen
of a native chief that he had ever met, and he had promised
to select a suitable locality for a mission station, and would
probably have used his great influence among his people on
the right side. But almost immediately after Livingstone's
arrival, when the way of salvation had been proclaimed to
him but once, Sebituane was seized with severe inflammation
of the lungs, and died after a fortnight's illness. Not being
permitted by the attendants to turn the dying man's thoughts
to his Father in Heaven, all Livingstone could do was to
commend his soul to God.

After several attempts, Dr. Livingstone saw no prospect of
obtaining a suitable station, and with great reluctance made
up his mind to retrace his weary way to Kolobeng. But these
journeys were not wholly useless. While making his first
journey, he discovered Lake N'gami, for which discovery he

received the prize for that year from the Royal Geographical Society. The journey which he made so successfully had hitherto baffled the best furnished travellers. The president of the society frankly ascribed Livingstone's success to the influence which he had acquired, as a missionary, among the natives. This the explorer himself also thoroughly believed, saying that the lake belonged to missionary enterprise. The river Zambesi was another of his discoveries at this time. On two of these journeys his wife and family accompanied him, and were mercifully preserved, though nearly dying on the way from the African fever.

Meantime, amid all his countless labors, Dr. Livingstone's mind was constantly busy with the scientific aspects of the country, and the great problem of its evangelization. Three things appeared to his mind essential to the successful solution of this problem, and he urged them constantly upon the directors. They were the vigorous pushing forward of the work into the interior, the employment of native agency, and the establishment of a training-school where such agency might be qualified.

At length it became certain that the tribe of the Bak- wains, among whom Livingstone had labored, must seek a new home. Added to the lack of rain was the threatening attitude of the Boers of the Transvaal, who hated Living- stone because of his attempts to christianize the natives, whom they regarded as without souls and made only to serve the white men, and who were seeking an occasion of quarrel as a pretext for breaking up the mission. It was plain that there was no hope of the Boers allowing the peaceable instruction of the natives at Kolobeng. When Sechele understood this, he sent his five children for instruction in all the knowledge of the white men to Dr. Moffat, at Kuruman, who kindly received them and their attendants into his own family.

Should Livingstone then seek some better location with this tribe among whom he had been laboring? His feeling in the matter is thus set forth: "If I were to follow my own inclinations, they would lead me to settle down quietly with the Bakwains, or some other small tribe, and devote some of my time to my children, but Providence seems to call me to the regions beyond." Friends urge him to remain, and doubtless had he been a man of only ordinary ability he would have done so, and in so acting would have done wisely. But his is a mind of larger scope. The great unevangelized interior of Africa beckons him on with irresistible power, and he dares not disobey what is beyond all doubt the call of God.

But this involves separation from his family. He dares not take them with him into that perilous fever country, while he again seeks a new and healthful site for the location of a mission station. Neither can he leave them alone among the natives, for fear of the disastrous influence upon his children. There is nothing for them to do but to return to England for the present, hoping to rejoin him at the end of two years.

And so they turn their backs upon Kolobeng. Sorrowfully must they have looked for the last time upon that African home; more sorrowfully still had they but known that they were never to be together in a home of their own again!

CHAPTER V.

AMONG THE MAKOLOLO.

AFTER accompanying his wife and children to the Cape, and there with a heavy heart bidding them farewell as they sailed for England, Dr. Livingstone turned his attention to preparations for a journey of 1,000 miles to the northward. In this he had three ends in view. First, the finding of a healthful location for a mission in the Barotse country, to which he could bring his family. Then as he realized that the distance from the Cape was too great to permit communication between the coast and the Barotse country by this route, he wished to find some passage to the coast, either east or west. Besides this, the shadow of the slave-trade was, as a new thing, beginning to darken that portion of the land to which he was going. In addition to the inhumanity of the slave-traffic, Livingstone saw that it would prove an insurmountable barrier in the way of missionary operations, but that while it was the only profitable traffic known to the natives they would not abandon it. It was of vital importance, therefore, to take steps for the introduction of some legitimate commerce by which the slave-trade might be supplanted.

Livingstone left the Cape in June, 1852, but owing to many annoying delays, it was September before he reached Kuruman. Here the sad news of the attack of the Boers on the Bakwains was brought to him by the wife of Sechele, who had herself been hidden in a cleft of the rock over which a number of the assailants were firing. The tribe of the Bakwains had already left Kolobeng and found a new home somewhat to the south.   The Boers had come first to the deserted station, where they showed their hatred of Livingstone by gutting his house, destroying his furniture and whatever they could lay their hands on, and tearing in pieces his precious books and journals.   Then they had followed the Bakwains to Limaue, where they had arrived on a Saturday evening, "spoiling for the fray."   They told Sechele that they had come to fight because he was getting "too saucy," allowing Englishmen to proceed to the north, though they had repeatedly ordered him not to do so.   To this the chief replied that he could not molest Englishmen, when they had never done him any harm, but had always treated him well.   Yielding to his earnest entreaties that they should not fight upon the Sabbath day, the Boers waited until Monday morning before beginning their assault.   Then they began firing upon the town and upon the Bakwains, who made a brave resistance all day, but were finally forced to retire on account of having no water.   Thirty-five Boers and sixty Bakwains were killed during the fight.   This village and others in the vicinity were set on fire by the Boers, the crops of the people burned, and their cattle carried off, all without the slightest provocation, but out of sheer hatred to the mission, and with the avowed determination to kill Livingstone had they found him, as they expected to do.   Had he been able to carry out his original intention of arriving at Kolobeng in August, he would probably have lost his life; or, had he escaped with that, at the least all the property that he carried with him for the journey would have been seized, and his projected enterprise brought to an end.

Dr. Livingstone did not hesitate to express his righteous indignation over the injustice and cruelty of the Boers.   For one ordinarily so patient, he had a very large vial of indignation which he poured out right heartily when he thought the occasion demanded it. The subsequent history of the Transvaal Republic did much to convince others that he was not far wrong as regards the low estimation in which he held these " free and independent " Boers.

As for Livingstone the effect of this outrage was to free him from the last local tie, and to give fresh vigor to his determination to open the country which the Boers were trying so hard to shut up. To his brother-in-law he wrote that he would open a path through the country, *or perish.*

In June, 1853, Livingstone had reached the Makololo country. His journal shows how unwearied were his efforts to teach the people, though, as was to be expected, they received ideas on divine subjects but slowly. All the Africans he met were firmly persuaded that they should have a future existence, and had also a vague kind of belief in some Supreme Being, but this was all, and as in our case at home, nothing less than the instructions and example of many years could be *depended* upon to secure their moral elevation. " We introduce," he writes, "entirely new motives, and were these not perfectly adapted for the human mind and heart by their divine Author, we should have no success. . . . We can afford to work in faith, for Omnipotence is pledged to fulfil the promise. . . . Our work and its fruits are cumulative; we work towards another state of things. Future missionaries will be rewarded by conversions for every sermon. We are their pioneers and helpers. Let them not forget the watchmen of the night — us, who worked when all was gloom, and no evidence of success in the way of conversion cheered our paths. They will doubtless have more light than we; but we served our Master earnestly, and proclaimed the same gospel as they will do."

In his endeavors to find a healthful locality Livingstone penetrated to the farthest limit of the Barotse country, but no such place as he sought could be found. Everywhere he finds the terrible African fever that had so nearly proved fatal to his own family on their previous journeys. Here, too, the horrors of the slave-trade haunt and harrow him, while he sees heathenism in its most unadulterated forms.

"During a nine weeks' tour," he says, "I had been in closer contact, with heathens than I had ever been before; and though all were as kind and attentive to me as possible, yet to endure the dancing, roaring, and singing, the jesting, grumbling, quarreling and murderings of these children of nature, was the severest penance I had yet undergone in the course of my missionary duties. I thence derived a more intense disgust of paganism than I had hitherto felt, and formed a greatly elevated opinion of the effects of missions in the south, among tribes which are reported to have been as savage as the Makololo. The benefits which to a casual observer may be inappreciable are worth all the money and labor that have been expended to produce them."

With respect to the results already obtained by the labors of missionaries he writes elsewhere: "Having visited Sierra Leone and some other parts of the West Coast, as well as a great part of South Africa, we were very much gratified by the evidences of success which came under our own personal observation. The crowds of well-dressed, devout and intelligent-looking worshipers, in both the west and south, formed a wonderful constrast to the same people still in their heathen state. At Sierra Leone, Kuruman, and other places, the Sunday, for instance, seemed as well observed as it is anywhere in Scotland." This is certainly more than can be said of our own land, though it must make us blush to acknowledge it. Indeed it is now said that in Sierra Leone there is a larger proportion of Christians than in the United States.

Of course Livingstone, travelling about from place to place as he did, was not cheered by such results as these which could only follow many years of seed-sowing; but amid all his difficulties, he patiently pursued his work as missionary, preaching twice every Sunday, generally to good audiences, sometimes to as many as a thousand. Sometimes he was greatly in hopes that a real impression had been made, but he was continually met by the notion that the Christian religion was a religion of medicines, and that all the good it could do was by charms.

"The great difficulty"—to quote again from his journals —"in dealing with these people is to make the subject plain. The minds of the auditors can not be understood by one who has not mingled much with them. They readily pray for the forgiveness of sin, and then sin again; confess the evil of it, and there the matter ends."

Sometimes, too, Livingstone experienced the disadvantage of having to speak through an interpreter. It was easy enough to carry on communication on all ordinary matters through the medium of a third person, but when it came to the exposition of religious truth, in which the interpreter took little or no interest, it was "uncommonly slow work." Some, indeed, began to pray to Jesus in secret as soon as they heard of the white man's God, but with little comprehension of what they were doing. Many, however, kept to the determination not to believe, like certain villagers in the south, who put all their cocks to death because they seemed to crow the words "Tlang lo rapeleng"—"Come along to prayers."

CHAPTER VI.

ACROSS THE CONTINENT.

SOME of Dr. Livingstone's friends thought that he should have settled somewhere, "preaching the simple gospel, and seeing conversions as the result of each sermon." To his father and other friends he writes in September, 1853: " The conversion of a few, however valuable their souls may be, can not be put into the scale against the knowledge of the truth spread over the whole country. In this I do and will exult. As in India, we are doomed to perpetual disappointment; but the knowledge of Christ spreads over the masses.   We are like voices crying in the wilderness; we prepare the way for the glorious future in which missionaries telling the same tale of love will convert by every sermon.   I am trying now to establish the Lord's kingdom in a region wider by far than Scotland. Fever seems to forbid, but I shall work for the glory of Christ's kingdom—fever or no fever."

Having been completely baffled in his search for a healthful location for mission work, Livingstone now turns his thoughts to the second object he has had in view, and endeavors to find a highway to the sea, pushing forward to the west coast.   The probability of his falling by the way is ever before him, but, as he often says, " Cannot the love of Christ carry the missionary where the slave trade carries the trader?"   So with a band of Makololo, the best natives with whom he ever travelled, he plunges boldly into the unknown country.

Yet even the best natives Livingstone finds ready to succumb to every trouble, and weak and helpless except as he infuses his own strength and courage into them. Of physical strength he himself had but little. During this terrible journey of seven months, from November 1853 to June 1854, he had thirty-one attacks of intermittent fever. The story of incredible hardships, sickness, hunger, constant wading through swollen streams, tedious delays, and harassing exactions of hostile tribes has been thrillingly told in Livingstone's first published *Travels* which made his name a household word in England and America.

When at last he reached the Portuguese settlement of St. Paul de Loanda on the coast, it was as a skeleton clothed in tatters, and he was soon prostrated by a long and distressing illness. But even this trial had its alleviations. He speaks of the delightful sensation of resting on a comfortable bed after so many months of lying upon the ground. The kind attentions of the Portuguese traders and others were also refreshing to the soul of the weary and lonely explorer.

When he had once more regained his strength he might have set sail immediately for England and his wife and children. The two years of absence had gone by, and great must have been the temptation to go to them at once. But he had promised the natives who had accompanied him that he would bring them back to their homes, and he knew that they were quite unable to perform that formidable journey without him. Besides, he had not yet accomplished his object. He had found no safe locality for a mission, nor any practicable highway to the sea. So once more he plunged into the wilderness, and with a repetition of his former hardships, and far more loss of time, brought his followers back to their homes.

It was his earnest desire to bring them *all* safely home, and in point of fact the whole twenty-seven returned in good health, notwithstanding all the perils of the way, owing largely, doubtless, to his careful oversight.   No wonder that his followers had an extraordinary regard for him.   Once when crossing a river the ox he was riding threw him off into the water, and at once about twenty of his men made a simultaneous rush for his rescue, and their joy at his safety was very great.

On his way back to the Barotse country Livingstone had a severe attack of rheumatic fever.   " I got it by sleeping in the wet," he says.   " There was no help for it.   Every part of a plain was flooded ankle deep.   We got soaked by going on, and sodden if we stood still."   The rain was often so drenching that he had to put his watch under his arm-pit to keep it dry.   His bed was on the wet grass with only a horse-cloth between to keep off a little of the dampness.   " It is true that I suffered severely from fever," he writes again, " but my experience cannot be taken as a fair criterion in the matter.   Compelled to sleep on the damp ground month after month, exposed to drenching showers, and getting the lower extremities wetted two or three times every day, living on manioc roots and meal, and exposed during many hours each day to the direct rays of the sun with the thermometer standing above 96° in the shade — these constitute a more pitiful hygiene than any succeeding missionaries will have to endure."

As they near the home of most of his followers matters brighten, and he writes: " Our progress down the Barotse valley was quite an ovation; the people were wonderfully kind, and every village gave us an ox and sometimes two.   I felt most deeply grateful, and tried to benefit them in the only way I could, by imparting the knowledge of that

Savior who alone can comfort them in the time of need, and of that good Spirit who alone can instruct them, and lead them into his kingdom." On arriving at their journey's end, a day of thanksgiving was observed. (July 23d, 1855.)

After a few months of rest, months in which, however, he did not fail to work and pray for the salvation of those about him, Livingstone set out once more on his weary way, — this time to the east coast, which seemed to promise better than the west. He followed the course of the Zambesi river, discovering the wonderful Victoria Falls, like a second Niagara, but grander and more astonishing. Two subjects that occupied much of his thoughts on these long journeys were the configuration of the country, and the best way of conducting missions and bringing the Africans to Christ.

On this journey he was often in extreme danger from the natives, but his trust in the Lord never faltered. "Travelling from day to day among barbarians," he himself says — and it is the universal testimony of those who have tried it — "exerts a most benumbing effect on the religious feelings of the soul," but his private journals show that through all the obstacles and trials that beset him he stood firmly upon the Rock, Christ Jesus.

When in imminent peril at the confluence of the Zambesi and Loangwa, he writes in his journal January 14, 1856: "Thank God for His great mercies thus far. How soon I may be called to stand before Him, my righteous Judge, I know not. All hearts are in His hands, and merciful and gracious is the Lord our God. O Jesus, grant me resignation to Thy will, and entire reliance on Thy powerful hand. On Thy word alone I lean. But wilt Thou permit me to plead for Africa? The cause is Thine. What an impulse will be

given to the idea that Africa is not open if I perish now!
See, O Lord, how the heathen rise up against me as they did
to Thy Son. I commit my way unto Thee; I trust also in
Thee that Thou wilt direct my steps. Thou givest wisdom
liberally to all who ask Thee — give it to me, my Father.
My family is Thine. They are in the best hands. Oh! be
gracious, and all our sins do Thou blot out.

> ' A guilty, weak and helpless worm
> On Thy kind arms I fall.'

Leave me not, forsake me not I cast myself and all my
cares down at Thy feet. Thou knowest all I need, for time
and for eternity."

At this time he had just made the discovery of two
healthy ridges at the mouth of the Loangwa, which had given
him new hope for missions and commerce; hence the special
earnestness with which he pleads that if the Lord will he
may be spared still longer to do his work. He was anxious
that others should know of his success in at last finding a
healthful locality, and cherished the earnest hope that the
directors would establish a mission there.

When he finally reached Quilimane, another Portuguese
settlement on the east coast, in May, 1856, a few days less
than four years from the time of his leaving the Cape had
elapsed. In this time he had crossed the entire continent —
a feat never before accomplished by a European — and that
amid hardships and dangers to which all but the bravest and
most persevering would have inevitably succumbed. That
his wonderful success as an explorer had not been unrecog-
nized is shown in the fact that in May, 1855, the Geographical Society had awarded him their gold medal — the highest
honor they had to bestow.

The Astronomer-royal at the Cape, Mr. Maclear, had said

of him: "He has done that which few other travellers in Africa can boast of: he has fixed his geographical points with very great accuracy, and yet he is only a poor missionary." But now as Dr. Livingstone once more emerges into civilized regions, he finds himself no longer the obscure missionary, but the world-renowned discoverer.

Let us not imagine, however, that he had lost anything of his missionary spirit in the zeal of the explorer. All through these journeys he had constantly preached the gospel to the various tribes through whose countries he passed. Even when too ill to hold his usual Sabbath services he would make use of a magic lantern, with pictures of Scripture scenes. He could thus convey important truths in a way particularly attractive to his rude audiences. Before he set out on this journey he wrote to his father: "I am a missionary, heart and soul. God had an only Son, and he was a missionary and a physician. A poor, poor imitation of Him I am, or wish to be. In this service I hope to live; in it I wish to die." And a sentence penned toward the close of his journey shows with what spirit it had been carried through. "Viewed in relation to my calling," he writes, "the end of the geographical feat is only the beginning of the enterprise."

CHAPTER VII.

FIRST VISIT TO ENGLAND.

WHILE still at Quilimane a communication received from the London Missionary Society disturbed Livingstone not a little. It informed him that the financial circumstances of the society were such that it could not venture to undertake untried any remote and difficult fields of labor. The Doctor naturally understood this to mean that his proposals were declined. He replied to the society's agent at Cape Town that he had thought that his preaching, conversation and travel were as nearly connected with the spread of the gospel as the Boers would allow them to be. His plan of opening up a path from either the east or the west coast had received the formal approbation of the directors, and in carrying it out he felt that he was doing good service to the cause of Christ. Seven times had he been in peril of his life from savage men, while laboriously pursuing that plan and never doubting that he was in the path of duty. He closes thus: "I shall not boast of what I have done; but the wonderful mercy I have received will constrain me to follow out the work in spite of the veto of the Board. If it is according to the will of God, means will be provided from other quarters."

Now at last Livingstone felt that he might revisit "dear old England," and after a long and perilous voyage he once more joyfully greeted his wife and children. But his joy was mingled with sadness, for the loved father whom he also longed to see was no more upon earth. While his son was on his way home he had departed "full of faith and peace." "You wished so much to see David," said his daughter to him as the end drew near. "Ay, very much, very much; but the will of the Lord be done." Then after a pause, "But I think I'll know whatever is worth knowing about him. When you see him, tell him I think so." When Livingstone returned to his childhood's home the sight of his father's empty chair deeply affected him. One of his sisters writes : "The first evening he asked all about his illness and death. One of us remarking that after he knew he was dying his spirits seemed to rise, David burst into tears. At family worship that evening he said with deep feeling, "We bless Thee, O Lord, for our parents; we give Thee thanks for the dead who has died in the Lord."

Besides the joy of being welcomed by those who were nearest and dearest to him, Dr. Livingstone now found himself welcomed to the society of the best and most eminent in the land, and the recipient of honors and distinctions innumerable. "Traveller, geographer, zoölogist, astronomer, missionary, physician and mercantile director, did ever man sustain so many characters at once? Or did ever man perform the duties of each with such pains-taking accuracy, and so great success?"

Having been urged to gather up the results of his journey and give them in the form of a book to the public, a large part of the year 1857 was mainly occupied with the labor of writing. Although he had ample material in his journals, the task of arrangement and transcription was necessarily very tedious. In fact Livingstone used to say that he would rather cross Africa than write another book! Complaint has sometimes been made that so much of this book is occupied with matters of science, descriptions of plants and animals, and geographical inquiries, and so little with what

directly concerns the work of the missionary. If the information given and the views expressed on missionary topics
were all put together they would constitute no insignificant
contribution to missionary literature. But Livingstone recognized himself as only a pioneer in missionary enterprise. Probably no missionary in Africa had preached to so many blacks,
but in most cases he had been a sower of seed, and not a
reaper of harvests. He had indeed been the instrument of
turning some from darkness to light, but he felt that the
missionary work of the interior of Africa was yet to be done.
By showing the vast fields ripe for the harvest he sought to
arouse the enthusiasm of Christian people, and lead them to
take possession of Africa for Christ. He wished to interest
men of science, men of commerce, men of all sorts in the
welfare of Africa. He would faithfully record what he
himself knew, and let others build with his materials. With
himself always " the end of the geographical feat is only the
beginning of the enterprise."

Busy and tired with the labors of authorship as he was,
this must have been one of the happiest periods of his life.
Often he worked with his children about him, undisturbed by
all their noise and play. After the years of loneliness which
he had passed, their mere presence must have been a satisfaction. Often he would walk and romp with them. A
favorite pastime with him when walking near the woods was
suddenly to plunge into the underbrush, and set them looking for him, as people searched for him afterwards when he
disappeared in Africa, and then as suddenly to reappear from
some entirely unexpected quarter.

Through the handsome conduct of his publishers and the
great success of the *Missionary Travels*, his book brought
him a small fortune, of which all that he thought it his duty

to reserve for his children was enough to educate them and prepare them for their part in life. A large portion of the profits went to forward directly the great object to which his heart and life had been already given.

Finding himself in the autumn of 1857 free from his labors as an author, Livingstone moved more freely through the country, attending meetings and giving addresses. It was, however, more from an appreciation of the kindness shown him, and a desire to be obliging, than from any wish to push himself forward, that he accepted these public invitations. He was anxious to return to his chosen life-work, and he was too modest a man to enjoy the lionizing which he so frequently received. But as long as the opportunity was given him he was glad to strive to arouse an interest in the evangelization of Africa, and to speak a word, as opportunity offered, for his Master.

It was in this year that he took a step which has often been severely criticised, viz., the severing of his connection with the London Missionary Society. Yet this was a thoroughly conscientious step, taken because he felt that God had called him to be a pioneer in the work of opening the continent of Africa, which might seem to many to be too remote from the immediate office of a missionary to warrant his receiving a salary from funds contributed solely for that work. He therefore thought it best to accept a position tendered him as consul, with government salary, at Quilimane, for the eastern coast and a portion of the interior of Africa, and also as commander of an expedition for exploring the eastern and central portions of the country. Yet while making these arrangements, he closed an impressive address at Cambridge with these words, following an earnest appeal that many of his hearers should enter upon missionary work themselves:

"If you knew the satisfaction of performing a duty as well as the gratitude to God which the missionary must always feel in being chosen for so noble and sacred a calling, you would have no hesitation in embracing it. For my own part I have never ceased to rejoice that God has appointed me to such an office. People talk of the sacrifice I have made in spending so much of my life in Africa. Can that be called a sacrifice which is simply paid back as a small part of a great debt owing to our God, which we can never repay? . . . Anxiety, sickness, suffering or danger now and then, with a foregoing of the common conveniences and charities of this life may make us pause and cause the spirit to waver, and the soul to sink; but let this only be for a moment. All these are nothing when compared with the glory which shall hereafter be revealed in and for us. I never made a sacrifice. Of this we ought not to talk when we remember the great sacrifice which *He* made who left His Father's throne on high to give Himself for us; 'who being the brightness of that Father's glory, and the express image of His person, and upholding all things by the word of His power, when He had by Himself purged our sins, sat down on the right hand of the Majesty on high.' . . . I beg to direct your attention to Africa; I know that in a few years I shall be cut off in that country which is now open; do not let it be shut again! I go back to Africa to make an open path for commerce and Christianity; do you carry out the work which I have begun. I LEAVE IT WITH YOU!"

In another address he says: "For my own part I go out as a missionary. . . . My object in Africa is not only the elevation of man, but that the country might be so opened that man might see the need of his soul's salvation." These words need no commentary.

Livingstone's visit to England, though comparatively short, taken in connection with his previous labors, had effected quite a revolution of ideas in regard to Africa. Men were surprised to find that instead of a great sandy desert it was so rich and productive a land. The impression had been quite general that the blacks were brutish and ferocious in a marked degree, but Livingstone showed, as Moffat had shown before him, that, rightly dealt with, they were teachable, affectionate, and the possessors of many good qualities. On the slave-trade of the interior he had already thrown a ghastly light, though in his later journeys he was still more impressed by its enormities. He had thrown light also on the structure of Africa, marking down his discoveries upon its map with the greatest accuracy. He had made appeals, too, in the cause of missions, with the effect of arousing considerable interest in them.

As for himself his heart yearned after his friends, the Makololo, and he would gladly have been their missionary, but as duty called him elsewhere he made an arrangement with his brother-in-law, Mr. John Moffat, to become their missionary instead, giving him an outfit and salary for five years out of his own private means. An amount was thus pledged and paid nearly equal to all the salary which he received as consul during three years.

CHAPTER VIII.

EXPEDITION TO THE ZAMBESI.

DR. LIVINGSTONE had told his faithful followers in Africa that nothing but death should prevent his returning to them, and he kept his word. In March, 1858, with his beloved wife, his youngest son, and the members of the expedition, he set sail from Liverpool. The steamer also carried the sections of a steam-launch, called *Ma Robert*, from Mrs. Livingstone's African name, meaning the mother of Robert, the eldest son. This boat it was hoped would be of the greatest use in the exploration of the Zambesi and its tributaries. Now at last the future seemed to open brightly before him. Ample funds were at his disposal, as well as a force adequate to all the demands of such an expedition. Instead of wearily tramping over the country he now had a little steamer to carry him where he liked, and last, but not least, his wife hoped not to leave him again.

But these bright hopes were not to be all realized. His first great disappointment occurred when on arriving at Cape Town the poor health of Mrs. Livingstone prevented her accompanying him further. She accordingly went to her parents at Kuruman, hoping at some future time to rejoin her husband on the Zambesi.

At first the expedition prospered in spite of some drawbacks. The remainder of 1858 and almost all of 1859 were occupied in exploring the Zambesi and its tributary, the Shiré. The discovery of the beautiful Lake Nyassa took place in September, 1859. From the very first, Livingstone saw the importance of this lake and the Shiré valley as the key to Central Africa. Since then it has been more and more evident that his opinion was correct. He thought much of the desirability of a British colony, and if twenty or thirty families from among the Scotch or English poor would come out as an experiment, he was ready to give £2000 towards the enterprise, without saying from whom the assistance came. He felt that the surest way to discourage the trade in slaves was to develop the trade in cotton, and that Christian families would do more to promote the cause of Christ among the natives than solitary missionaries could do. The configuration of the Shiré valley is particularly favorable for colonization, three broad plateaus rising from the river, one above another, to the height of 5,000 feet. As to the fertility of the land, the statement was made in 1887 that while of three coffee plants taken out to the Shiré hills eight years before from the Edinburgh Botanic Gardens only one had survived, the fruits of that one had already amounted to seventy bags of many hundred weight, and of the finest growth. "The culture is a commercial success," says the organ of the present Universities' Mission, "and should result in time in covering all the hills and plateaus around the lake with this best foe of the slave-trade, and best substitute for the fast disappearing ivory."

But to go back to our expedition, the *Ma Robert*, which had promised so well at first, soon disappointed them greatly. Her consumption of coal was enormous, the furnace had to be started hours before the steam was serviceable, she snorted so horribly that she was called "The Asthmatic," and, after all, canoes could easily pass her when she was making her utmost speed. Dr. Livingstone was greatly mortified to find that he had been deceived. He had

4

thought that he was getting a great bargain, because the ship-builder had professed to do so much through "love of the cause."

We can have little idea of the trials of such an expedition even at its best. Now the heat and the mosquitoes, the delays, the stoppages on sandbanks, the almost incredible struggle for fuel —Livingstone writes that it took all hands a day and a half to cut one day's fuel — the monotony of existence, the malarious climate, the frequent attacks of illness, all had a most trying effect; "Very curious," writes Livingstone, "are the effects of African fever on certain minds. Cheerfulness vanishes, and the whole mental horizon is overcast with black clouds of gloom. The liveliest joke cannot provoke even the semblance of a smile. Nothing is right; nothing pleases the fever-stricken victim."

The commander had difficulties also in managing his own countrymen which he did not have with the natives. He was so conscientious, so thoroughly in earnest himself, that he could endure nothing that seemed like trifling with duty.

Travelling, even in a civilized country and surrounded by all the conveniences and even luxuries at the service of the modern tourist, is said to be peculiarly apt to bring out the disagreeable traits in one's character. But those who continued to enjoy his friendship never wearied of speaking of Livingstone's delightful qualities as a companion in travel, and of the warm sunshine which he had the faculty of spreading about him.

It is not often that Dr. Livingstone speaks of the delicacies of his table, but once on this trip so novel a dish is served up that he has to tell us about it.

"June, 1859. We had been very abundantly supplied with first-rate stores, but we were unfortunate enough to lose a considerable portion of them, and had now to bear the privation as best we could. On the way down we purchased a few gigantic cabbages and pumpkins at a native village below Mazaro. Our dinners had usually consisted of but a single course, but we were surprised the next day by our black cook from Sierra Leone bearing in a second course. 'What have you got there?' was asked in wonder. 'A tart, sir.' 'A tart! Of what is it made?' 'Of cabbages, sir.' As we had no sugar, and could not 'make believe' as in the days of boyhood, we did not enjoy the feast that Tom's genius had prepared."

Wherever he goes Dr. Livingstone studies the trees, plants and fruits of the region with a view to commerce. He is no less interested to watch the treatment of fever when cases occur, and is gratified to observe the efficacy of medicines of his own preparation.

Once he has an escape from a rhinoceros as remarkable as that from the lion. The animal came dashing at him, and suddenly stopped from some unknown reason when close to him, giving him time to escape. Apparently the unwonted sight of a white man had filled the beast with astonishment, and quite destroyed his presence of mind.

Coming among his old friends, the Makololo, in 1860, their expressions of kindness and confidence greatly touched him. But this confidence was wholly the result of his way of treating them. "It ought never to be forgotten," says he, "that influence among the heathen can be acquired only by patient continuance in well-doing, and that good manners are as necessary among barbarians as among the civilized." Such was his theory, and such no less his practice. He, too, could have confidence in them, as appears from the fact that he found on his return to Linyanti that the wagons and other articles which he had left there seven years before had been untouched, save by the weather and the white ants.

While among these people Livingstone labored unwea-riedly for their spiritual good. The last subject on which he preached to them at this time was the great resurrection. They told him that they could not believe it possible that the particles of the body should ever be reünited. Dr. Living-stone gave them in reply a chemical illustration, and then referred to the authority of the Book from which the doc-trine was derived; and the poor people were more willing to give in to the authority of the Bible than to the chemical illustration. Here, as always, the reference to the truth of the Bible and its Author seemed to have far more influence over the native mind than any cleverness of illustration, though that doubtless, too, had a certain weight of its own.

CHAPTER IX.

DEATH OF MRS. LIVINGSTONE.

AT THE beginning of 1861 a new steamer, the *Pioneer*, arrived, which, though not altogether satisfactory, was yet a great improvement on the *Ma Robert*, which was now totally useless. This boat was given by the English government for the navigation of the Zambesi and Shiré, and it carried the sections of the *Lady Nyassa*, designed to float on the waters of Lake Nyassa, and bought by Livingstone at the cost of £6,000, the greater part of the profits of his book.

During this year he explored the River Rovuma, and assisted Bishop Mackenzie and his co-laborers to establish the Universities' Mission on the Shiré, organized in response to a personal appeal from Livingstone to the English universities. The bishop was a man after Livingstone's own heart, and the mission was opened with the brightest hopes of success, doomed, alas, to speedy disappointment. This mission was ere long virtually, though not absolutely, broken up by the death of Bishop Mackenzie and several of his most efficient coworkers. This was a terrible blow to Dr. Livingstone, but it was followed by one still heavier, the death of his wife.

Early in January, 1862, Livingstone's wife was once more at his side, after an absence of four years. After returning to her children in Scotland, where she spent a year of great loneliness and depression, and intense longing for her husband, she had come back to Africa and rejoined him on the little steamer on the Zambesi, with bright plans for a happy home on the Nyassa.

Only three short months, however, were they together
before his wife was taken from him. After an illness of a
few days only, her spirit passed away, and the man who had
faced calmly so many deaths, and braved so many dangers,
knelt by her death-bed utterly broken down, and weeping
like a child.

Livingstone says little in his next book, *The Zambesi and
its Tributaries*, of the death of his wife. He cannot publish
to the world the deepest feelings of his heart, but his journals give us some inkling of what he suffered in her loss.
" It is the first heavy stroke I have suffered, and quite takes
away my strength. I wept over her who well deserved many
tears. I loved her when I married her, and the longer I lived
with her I loved her the more. God pity the poor children,
who were all tenderly attached to her; and I am left alone in
the world by one whom I felt to be a part of myself. I hope
it may, by divine grace, lead me to realize heaven as my
home, and that she has but preceded me in the journey, Oh,
my Mary, my Mary ! how often we have longed for a quiet
home since you and I were cast adrift at Kolobeng. Surely
the removal by a kind Father who knoweth our frame means
that He rewarded you by taking you to the best home, the
eternal one in the heavens. . . . For the first time in my
life I feel willing to die."

In a letter written two days after Mrs. Livingstone's death
he says: " This heavy stroke quite takes the heart out of me.
. . . I try to bend to the blow as from our heavenly
Father. . . I shall do my duty ; but it is with a darkened
horizon that I set about it."

A pleasant little glimpse of home life is given in a later
entry in his journal: " The loss of my ever dear Mary lies
like a heavy weight on my heart. In our intercourse in

private there was often more than what would be tnought by
some a decorous amount of merriment and play.   I said to
her a few days before her fatal illness: 'We old bodies
ought now to be more sober, and not play so much.' 'Oh
no,' said she, 'you must always be as playful as you have
always been.   I would not like you to be as grave as some
folks I have seen.'   This when I know her prayer was that
she might be spared to be a help and comfort to me in my
great work, led me to feel what I have always believed to be
the true way, to let the head grow wise, but keep the heart
always young and playful.   She was ready and anxious to
work, but has been called away to serve God in a higher
sphere."

The days after his wife's death were spent by Dr. Livingstone in writing fully to his children and family friends in
regard to his great loss.   His letter to his wife's mother,
Mrs. Moffat, reached her at Kuruman by way of England.
The sad tidings first came to her through traders, but before
the news came she had written a long letter to her daughter,
full of joy and gratitude that she and her husband had been
permitted to meet again, and full of bright hopes for their
future.   For a whole month before this letter was written
poor Mary had been sleeping under the baobab tree at Shu-
panga!

It is sad to read that, in addition to all their other trials,
Livingstone and his wife had not been able to escape the
tongue of slander.   In his letter to his mother-in-law is this
allusion: "I regret, as there are always regrets after one's
loved ones are gone, that the slander, which unfortunately
reached her ears from missionary gossips and others, had an
influence on me in allowing her to come before we were
fairly on Lake Nyassa.   A doctor of divinity said, when her

devotion to her family was praised: 'Oh, she is no good; she is here because her husband cannot live with her.' The last day will tell another tale."

Mrs. Moffat in her reply says: "As for the cruel scandal that seems to have hurt you both so much, those who said it did not know you *as a couple*.   In all *our* intercourse with you, we never had a doubt as to your being comfortable together.   I know there are some maudlin ladies who insinuate when a man leaves his family frequently, no matter how noble is his object, that he is not *comfortable* at home.   But we can afford to smile at this and say: 'The day will declare it.'"

To his daughter Agnes, after the account of her mother's death Livingstone writes: "Dear Nannie, she often thought of you, and when once from the violence of the disease she was delirious, she called out; 'See, Agnes is falling down a precipice.'   May our Heavenly Savior, who must be your father and guide, preserve you from falling into the gulf of sin over the precipice of temptation. . . Dear Agnes, I feel alone in the world now, and what will the poor dear baby do without her mamma? She often spoke of her and sometimes burst into a flood of tears, just as I now do in taking up and arranging the things left by my beloved partner of eighteen years. . . I bow to the divine hand that chastens me. God grant that I may learn the lesson He means to teach! All she told you to do she now enforces, as if beckoning from heaven.   Nannie dear, meet her there.   Don't lose the crown of joy she now wears, and the Lord be gracious to you in all things. . . I pity you on receiving this; but it is the Lord. Your sorrowing and lonely father."

Letters of like tenor were written to every intimate friend.   Livingstone's heart seemed to find relief in pouring itself out in praise of her whom he loved so dearly, and whom he should see no more on earth. How he must have yearned in this time of desolation for the comfort of the human sympathy, the clasp of the loving hands, of those dear to him, thousands of miles away. But He who alone can give true comfort, and who is just as near to His followers in the jungles of Africa as in the peaceful homes of England and America, gave him His peace, and courage to keep on his way, lonely yet undaunted, "faint yet pursuing."

CHAPTER X.

THE SLAVE-TRADE.

IT could not have been easy for Dr. Livingstone to take
up his work again, but how he was able to do it at all
may be inferred from these words, written at the time to his
friend, Rev. Mr. Waller, of the Universities' Mission:
"Thanks for your kind sympathy. In return, I say, cherish
exalted thoughts of the great work you have undertaken.
It is a work which, if faithful, you will look back on with
satisfaction while the eternal ages roll on their everlasting
course. The devil will do all he can to hinder you by efforts
from without and from within, but remember Him who is
with you, and will be with you alway."

As soon as he was able to brace himself for his work, he
undertook the task of helping to put the *Lady Nyassa*
together, and to launch her. This was achieved about the
last of June, 1862, to the great astonishment of the natives,
who could not comprehend how iron should float. This was
an excellent steamboat, and could she have been got to the
lake would have done well. But unhappily the rainy season
had passed, and this could not now be accomplished until
December. Here was another great disappointment. In the
meantime Livingstone again took up the explorations in
which he had been engaged when he went with Bishop
Mackenzie to help him settle. He hoped to find a water-way
to Nyassa beyond the dominion of the Portuguese, but
failed. It appeared best to reach the lake by the Zambesi
and Shiré, but it was not until early in 1863 that they were

able to renew the ascent of these rivers, with the *Lady Nyassa* in tow.

Dr. Livingstone had seen from the very outset the necessity of securing the coöperation of the Portuguese, who were in possession of the coast at the mouth of the Zambesi, and he had succeeded in obtaining from the king of Portugal the amplest assurances of sympathy and aid. Public instructions had been given to all Portuguese officials in Africa that all needful help should be given him. The actual policy of these officials was, however, quite the reverse of this, and they seemed bent upon thwarting in every possible way his noble endeavors to suppress that infamous traffic which brought them their wealth. Still more than this, it seemed as if his labors, instead of suppressing this terrible slave-trade, were actually helping it forward. As fast as he opened up the country slave-traders followed in his track, sometimes gaining the confidence of the unsuspecting natives by saying that they were Livingstone's children !

Now as the exploring party ascended the river the desolation was heart-breaking. Corpses floated past them in such numbers that the paddle-wheels had to be cleared from them every morning. "Wherever we took a walk, human skeletons were seen in every direction, and it was painfully interesting to observe the different postures in which the poor wretches had breathed their last. . . Many had ended their misery under shady trees, others under projecting crags in the hills, while others lay in their huts with closed doors, which when opened disclosed the mouldering corpse with the poor rags around the loins, the skull fallen off the pillow, the little skeleton of the child, that had perished first, rolled up in a mat between two large skeletons. The sight of this desert, but eighteen months ago a well-peopled valley, now

literally strewn with human bones, forced the conviction
upon us that the destruction of human life in the middle
passage, however great, constitutes but a small portion of the
waste, and made us feel that unless the slave-trade — that
monster iniquity which has so long brooded over Africa — is
put down, lawful commerce cannot be established."

At first Dr. Livingstone had been somewhat inclined to
think that the enormities of the slave-trade were sometimes
exaggerated. · Now he was convinced that they were
" beyond exaggeration."

Sometimes he was able to set the captives free, as on the
journey to Loanda, which was begun by a blessed act of
humanity, as he boldly summoned a trader to release a band
of captives, so that eighteen souls were restored to freedom
who else would have been miserable slaves.   On another
occasion, also previous to this time, he and his companions
had rescued a slave-party of manacled men, women and children.   Each man had his neck in the fork of a stout
stick six or seven feet long, and kept in by an iron rod riveted
at both ends across the throat.   With a saw one by one the
men were sawed out into freedom.   Many of the party were
children about five years old or even less.   Two women had
been shot the day before for attempting to untie the thongs,
in order that the rest might be intimidated; one woman had
had her infant's brains knocked out because she could not
carry both it and her load, and a man was despatched with
an axe because he had broken down with fatigue.   Eighty-
four, chiefly women and children, were set free; and on
being told that they might go where they pleased, or remain
with their liberators, they all chose to stay; and the bishop
wisely attached them to the mission, then just opened, to be
educated as members of a Christian family.   In this way a

great difficulty in the establishment of a mission was over-
come, for years are usually required to instil such confidence
into the natives' minds as to induce them — in any large
numbers at least — to submit to the guidance of strangers.

But while the release of slaves on their way to the coast
was sometimes effected, more frequently either it could not
be accomplished, or it was felt to be unwise, as the helpless
victims of the slave-agent were likely, if rescued, to fall again
into his pitiless hands, when their last state would inevitably
be worse than their first.

A few extracts from Livingstone's books, *The Zambesi
and its Tributaries* and the *Last Journals*, will give added
reason for his intense feeling on this subject:

"The assertion has been risked, because no one was in a
condition to deny it, that the slave-trade was like any other
branch of commerce, subject to the law of supply and
demand, and that therefore it ought to be free. From what
we have seen, it involves so much of murder in it as an essential element, that it can scarcely be allowed to remain in the
catalogue of commerce, any more than garroting, thuggee,
or piracy."

"June 26th, 1866.— We passed a slave woman shot or
stabbed through the body, and lying on the path. It was
said an Arab who passed early that morning had done it in
anger at losing the price he had given for her, because she
was unable to walk any longer."

"June 27th.— To-day we came upon a man dead from
starvation, as he was very thin. One of our men wandered
and found a number of slaves with slave-sticks on, abandoned
by their master for want of food. They were too weak to
be able to speak or say where they had come from; some
were quite young."

'Not more than one in five ever reach the 'kind masters' in Cuba and elsewhere, whom, according to slave-owners' interpretation of Scripture, Providence intended for them."

"We had a long discussion about the slave-trade. The Arabs have told the chief that our object in capturing slaves is to get them into our own possession and make them of our own religion. The evils which we have seen, the skulls, the ruined villages, the numbers who perish on the way to the coast and on the sea, the wholesale murders committed by the Waiyau to build up Arab villages elsewhere — these things Mukaté often tried to turn off with a laugh, but our remarks are safely lodged in many hearts. Next day, as we went along, our guides spontaneously delivered their substance to the different villages along our route. . . . It is but little we can do; but we lodge a protest in the heart against a vile system, and time may ripen it. Their great argument is: 'What could we do without Arab cloth?' My answer is: 'Do what you did before the Arabs came into the country.' At the present rate of destruction of population, the whole country will soon be a desert."

"The strangest disease I have seen in this country seems really to be broken-heartedness, and it attacks free men who have been captured and made slaves. Speaking with many who died from it, they ascribed their only pain to the heart, and placed the hand correctly on the spot, though many think that the organ stands high up under the breast-bone Some slavers expressed surprise to me that they should die, seeing they had plenty to eat and no work. . . . It seems to be really broken hearts of which they die."

Dr. Livingstone's servants afterwards said in answer to questions, that the sufferings of these captives were terrible. Many died because it was impossible for them to carry a burden on the head while marching in the heavy yoke, which weighs usually from thirty to forty pounds. Children for a time would keep up with wonderful endurance; but sometimes the sound of dancing and the merry tinkle of the small drums would fall on their ears in passing near to a village; then the memory of home and happy days proved too much for them; they cried and sobbed, the "broken heart" came on, and they rapidly sank. The adults, as a rule, never had been slaves before, and were so now only through treachery. The Arabs would often promise a present to villagers if they would act as guides to some distant point. As soon as they were far enough from their friends, they were seized and pinned into the slave-sticks, or yokes, from which there was no escape. These poor fellows would die, as stated above, talking to the last of their wives and children, who would never know what became of them.

Much more might be quoted in regard to this fearful traffic in humanity, but one more extract will suffice: "When endeavoring to give some account of the slave-trade of East Africa, it was necessary to keep far within the truth, in order not to be thought guilty of exaggeration, but, in sober seriousness, the subject does not admit of exaggeration. To overdraw its evils is a simple impossibility. The sights I have seen, though common incidents of the traffic, are so nauseous that I always strive to drive them from memory. In the case of most disagreeable recollections I can succeed, in time, in consigning them to oblivion; but the slavery scenes come back unbidden, and make me start up at night, horrified by their vividness."

CHAPTER XI.

RECALL, AND LAST VISIT TO ENGLAND.

D R. LIVINGSTONE'S heart was saddened also by the further news from the mission that several more of the missionaries had succumbed to the African fever. Of his own party some were so reduced by illness that they had to return to England, and now there were but two Europeans in it besides himself. We do not need to dwell on the noble spirit shown by Livingstone in remaining in the country in loneliness and sorrow, amid such appalling scenes as everywhere met him. His devotion to duty in spite of every obstacle, speaks for itself.

At the Murchison cataracts the *Lady Nyassa* was taken to pieces, while the party began to construct a road around the thirty-five or forty miles of the rapids, in order to convey the steamer to the lake. But before this work was completed Livingstone received a dispatch from Earl Russell, recalling the expedition. Of course this was a great disappointment, though not altogether a surprise. The reasons given for the recall of the expedition were that, though not through any fault of Dr. Livingstone's, it had not accomplished the objects for which it had been designed, and that it had proved much more costly than had been originally expected. Perhaps, too, the government felt that its remonstrances with the Portuguese government were of no avail, and that their relations were becoming too uncomfortable.

It was unfortunate that this recall should have occurred before Livingstone had been able to place the steamer, on which he had spent half his fortune, on Lake Nyassa. He had hoped that the British government would at least partially reimburse him for this outlay, but it was never done.

At no previous time had Livingstone been so completely hemmed in by discouragements as now. The expedition had been recalled, and his hopes of seeing the *Lady Nyassa* floating on the waters of the lake had been brought to an end; he had been grievously afflicted in the death of Bishop Mackenzie and his associates, and had received a still more crushing blow in the loss of his wife; disease had wasted and depressed him; he had had disappointments and delays without number, and apparently all his efforts to do good had been turned to evil. But, undeterred by all these troubles, he resolved to take the last opportunity of exploring the banks of the Nyassa, even if it could only be by the wearisome process of "trudge-trudging." Why should he not go home, and seek in the companionship of his children and friends the comfort and the rest that he needed? A single sentence in a letter to a friend, written while the recall was only in contemplation, explains why: "In my case duty would not lead me home, and home, therefore, I would not go."

So, with a small company of attendants, Livingstone sets out to visit the northern end of the lake, and if possible, to reach Lake Moero, of which he had heard as lying at some distance to the west. But this object he is unable to accomplish, as they are detained by illness, and he has not sufficient time at his disposal, the strict orders of government being that he must get the *Pioneer* down to the sea while the river is in flood. A month or six weeks more would have enabled him to finish his researches, but he does not dare to take the risk. On reaching the vessel, however, in November, 1863, he finds, to his intense chagrin, that two months have to be

5

spent waiting for the flood. As usual, though, he endeavors
to make the best of an unpleasant situation. "The first fortnight after our return to the ship," he writes, "was employed
in the delightful process of resting, to appreciate which a man
must have gone through great exertions. In our case the
muscles of the limbs were as hard as boards, and not an ounce
of fat existed on any part of the body."

While waiting here he received a letter from Bishop
Tozer, the successor of Bishop Mackenzie at the mission,
telling him that he had resolved to abandon the station, and
transfer operations to Zanzibar. Against this Livingstone
protested, but without avail, and thus, for his lifetime, ended
the Universities' Mission on the Shiré, with all the bright
hopes which it had inspired. This, he writes, he feels much
more than the recall of the expedition. When he thinks of
it, it seems as if he must "sit down and cry." Notwithstanding all that has been said against it, he believes that the
climate is a favorable one for mission enterprise, and he
would himself go and plant the gospel there were he only
younger. He believes that it will be done some day without
fail, though he may not live to see it. How his hopes were
finally realized we shall see a little farther on.

When, as Livingstone tells us, his patience was well-nigh
exhausted, the river rose, and he gladly started down the
Shiré in the *Pioneer*, with the *Lady Nyassa* in tow. On
the way they had at one time to spend the night in a marsh
where the water was as black as ink, and emitted such an
odor of sulphuretted hydrogen as to make the air most offen-
sive. Happily no ill effects followed, though fever was
feared. The next morning every particle of white paint on
both ships was so blackened that scrubbing with soap and
water could not clean it. The brass was all turned to a

bronze color, and even the iron and ropes had taken on a new tint. They tarried in the foul and blackening emanations from the marsh to receive on board about thirty poor orphans, and a few helpless widows, whom Bishop Mackenzie had attached to the mission. The bishop had formed a little free community in connection with the mission, in which all who had been able to support themselves by cultivating the soil had been encouraged to do so; but now that the mission had been given up, these little and helpless ones could not be abandoned without casting odium upon the English name, and bringing reproach upon the cause of Christ, and so they were carried to the Cape and cared for there. Mr. R. M. Ballantyne tells us that he found some years afterwards among the most efficient teachers in St. George's Orphanage, Cape Town, one of these black girls named Dauma, whom Bishop Mackenzie had personally rescued from the slaves and carried on his shoulders, and whom now Doctor Livingstone rescued a second time.

This experience in the marsh certainly does not give one a very favorable impression of the healthfulness of the locality, but we must remember that it was the Shiré *heights* that had been supposed to be particularly adapted to a mission station. From this more bracing climate the missionaries had unfortunately been driven by famine to the fertile but fever-smitten valley below.

The work of the mission as carried on at Zanzibar nas been chiefly with the great numbers of slaves rescued on the high seas by British cruisers. These on being brought back have been trained and taught before being sent inland to their homes. A great work has been done also in translating the Bible into different dialects; and on the site of the old slave-market of Zanzibar, once one of the vilest spots on earth,

tnere now stands a fine church, a fitting memorial of what has
been accomplished.   But the desire of Livingstone's heart
that the blessings of the gospel should be carried to the
people scattered about Lake Nyassa, as was the original
purpose of the Mission, was at last to be realized, though
too late for him to behold it except by the eye of faith ;
unless, indeed, he has been permitted to look down from the
"heavenly battlements" upon the work which was begun
under his inspiration.

In 1876 a settlement was made in the Nyassa region by a
missionary and sixty freed slaves from the training-school at
Zanzibar.   Others have since joined him, and besides spreading a knowledge of the gospel, the mission has done most
efficient service in checking the slave-traffic, having established a chain of stations along the old slave-trade routes
from Lake Nyassa to the sea.   A missionary steamer on the
lake proves of constant service.   A third branch of the Universities' Mission is maintained in the Rovuma district. The
present force of European workers numbers sixty-two, about
half of whom are artisans pursuing their several crafts, all,
however, actuated by the same purpose of consecration to the
Lord's work.

On reaching Mozambique the *Pioneer* was delivered over
to the navy, being the property of the English government.
Doctor Livingstone's plan was now to sail to India and sell
the *Lady Nyassa* before returning home.   "The Portuguese
would have bought her to use as a slaver," he wrote in a
letter to his daughter, "but I would rather see her go down
to the depths of the Indian Ocean than that."

His engineer left him for a better situation on reaching
Zanzibar, so Livingstone had to take charge himself, and to
navigate his vessel from Zanzibar to Bombay, a distance of

2500 miles with a crew of three Europeans and seven natives who had never before seen the ocean, and most of whom were disabled by illness during the voyage.   For forty-five days he was on an ocean he had never crossed, for twenty-five of which his vessel was becalmed.   The voyage was a memorable one, but has been so far eclipsed by the still greater wonders performed by the great explorer on land that little has been heard of it.

Upon reaching Bombay he sold his ship for a third of what it had cost him, and then sailed for England.   So ended in disappointment and seeming defeat this third period of his African life,

CHAPTER XII.

SEARCH FOR THE NILE SOURCES.

DR. LIVINGSTONE now feels that his immediate efforts must be directed towards rousing such a public sentiment against the Portuguese slave-trade that it shall be as perilous upon land as English ships have already made it upon the ocean. But the hope of obtaining access to the heart of Africa by another route than that of the Portuguese settlements is still in his heart, and as soon as possible he will return to look for a new route to the interior.

On arriving in England he spent a year upon his book, *The Zambesi and its Tributaries.* His intention was at first merely to write a small volume, a blast of the trumpet against the monstrous iniquity of the Portuguese slave-trade, but gradually it swelled to a goodly octavo, and embraced the history of the Zambesi expedition. The name of Charles Livingstone also appears on the title-page, his brother of that name having been with him part of the time during this expedition, and his journals having been made use of in the writing of the book.

Besides this work Dr. Livingstone did not fail to make use of such public opportunities as must come to a now famous explorer, in pleading for Africa.

It was the desire of his friend, Sir Roderick Murchison, by whom he was greatly influenced, that he should now completely lay aside his missionary character, and devote himself altogether to the geographical problem of determin-

ing the water-shed of the continent, and the true sources of
the Nile. We can see how Livingstone regarded this propo-
sition by a significant entry in his journal of January 7th,
1865 : "Answered Sir Roderick about going out. Said I
could only feel in the way of duty by working as a missionary." It did fall in with his intentions, however, to
explore the region in which he believed the sources of the
Nile would be found, and he therefore entered into an agree-
ment with the Geographical Society to undertake, as a part
of his work, the task of determining the water-shed of
central Africa. For this he received a grant of £500 from
the society, another of the same amount from the government,
and the honor of a Consul's title *without salary*. For most
of the expense incidental to so great an undertaking he must
rely upon his own means, or trust to Providence.

In June of this year he paid " the last tribute to a dear,
good mother," helping to lay her in the grave, as she had
wished he might.

Before leaving Scotland Livingstone made a little speech
to some school-children, closing with what had been the
watch-word of his own life, " Fear God and work hard."
These were the last public words that he ever uttered in his
native country.

Quitting England in the autumn of 1865, he left Zanzibar to enter Africa for the last time on March 19th, 1866,
his fifty-third birthday. " I set out on this journey," he
observes, " with a strong presentiment that I should never
finish it. The feeling did not interfere with me in reference
to my duty, but it made me think a great deal of the future
state, and come to the conclusion that possibly the change
is not so great as we have usually believed. The appearances
of Him who is all in all to us were especially human ; and

the prophet whom St. John wanted to worship had work to
do, just as we have, and did it."

Our explorer chooses, this time, to have no white companions, but takes with him such a retinue of black attendants
as is necessary for the journey. Eight of them are young
liberated slaves from the missionary school at Nassick, near
Bombay, some of whom displayed such fidelity to their
master in life and death as to win the admiration of the
world. But they were supplemented at Zanzibar by Johanna
men and sepoys, the former of whom were thieves, and the
latter so intolerable that Livingstone soon dismissed them
altogether, and detachments subsequently sent to him proved
to be no better.

The exploring party dived into the depths of the
unknown continent, and for months nothing was heard of
them. Finally one of the Johanna men arrived at Zanzibar
with circumstantial news that Dr. Livingstone had been
murdered on the shores of Lake Nyassa. Unwilling to go
any farther with the party, and freely permitted to return,
he had invented this story to cover his own desertion.
Although the newspapers were full of obituary notices, the
report was only half-credited in England, and to relieve the
suspense a search-party was sent out in quest of him.
Although not finding Dr. Livingstone, they gained abundant
evidence that the story was false, and in 1868 letters came
from the missionary himself, telling of the desertion of the
Johanna men, and of the discovery of Lakes Moero and
Bangweolo.

We may learn something of the trials he experienced,
and of his life in general in the meantime, by the following
extracts from the journals which were entrusted to Stanley
when he left him.

January 20th, '67, after telling how two of the men had deserted, taking what could least be spared, the medicine-box, which was undoubtedly thrown away as soon as they came to examine their booty, he adds, "I felt as if I had now received the sentence of death, like poor Bishop Mackenzie." The bishop had had all his drugs destroyed by the upsetting of a canoe in which was his case of medicines, and without these had speedily succumbed to the dreaded African fever. In Dr. Livingstone's case also the loss of his medicines was probably the beginning of the end, and his system lost the wonderful power of recovery it had hitherto shown.

"January 27th. In changing my dress this A. M. I was frightened at my own emaciation."

"April 1st, '67. I am excessively weak; can not walk without tottering, and have constant singing in the head, but the Highest will lead me farther. . . . After I had been a few days here I had a fit of insensibility, which shows the power of fever without medicine. I found myself floundering outside my hut, and, unable to get in, I tried to lift myself from my back by laying hold of two posts at the entrance, but when I got nearly upright I let them go, and fell back heavily on my head on a box. The boys had seen the wretched state I was in, and hung a blanket at the entrance of the hut, that no strangers might see my helplessness ; some hours elapsed before I could recognize where I was."

Besides suffering from the loss of his medicine-chest, Livingstone was really half-starved. He had no tea, coffee, or sugar, and hardly anything to eat except a coarse, tasteless kind of African maize, a most unsatisfying food, which left him constantly hungry.

The two geographical feats of the year 1867 were the discovery of Lake Moero, and the first sight of Lake Tanganyika. In 1868 he thus quietly records the discovery of Lake Bangweolo. "On the 18th of July I walked a little way out, and saw the shores of the lake for the first time, thankful that I had come safely hither."

New Year's day, 1869, found Livingstone laboring under a more severe attack of illness than any he had heretofore experienced. .

Six weeks of pneumonia left evils behind from which he never fully recovered. So ill was he that he completely lost count of the days of the week and month. Writing of this experience, he says: "I saw myself lying dead in the way to Ujiji. . . . When I think of my children the lines ring through my head perpetually:

"I shall look into your faces,
    And listen to what you say;
And be often very near you,
    When you think I'm far away."

In addition to his other trials, it happened again and again, that after wearily marching scores, or even hundreds of miles to reach new supplies ordered from the coast, it was only to find his stores broken open by the faithless natives, his goods scattered far and wide, and even his letters lost. Truly in such circumstances one had need of an almost infinite patience, but patient, quiet endurance was one of Livingstone's strong points.

Then to all this must be added the trial of hope deferred, as repeatedly the key to the problem he was endeavoring to solve seemed to be almost within reach, only to elude him after all. Perhaps if he had foreseen the difficulties of the enterprise, he might not have deemed it worth the price it

cost; but he had given his promise to the Geographical
Society, and, as we have seen, he was a man not easily daunt-
ed. Moreover he had a strong impression that if he could
only find the real sources of the Nile, he could acquire such
influence that new weight would be given to his pleadings
for Africa.

Wherever he went, he had some opportunities to make
known God's love as manifested in His only Son, although the
seed sown seemed seldom to take root. He was also constantly gaining fresh information in regard to the country
and the slave-trade.

Five weary years from 1866 to 1871 were thus spent in
traversing back and forth the basins of Lakes Nyassa, Tanganyika, Moero and Bangweolo, one year after another being
begun with the pathetic prayer that *this* year he might be permitted to finish his task and go home. Many difficulties
surrounded him; massacres and atrocities were of frequent
occurrence; the Arab slave-dealers thwarted him whenever
it was possible; his feet were lacerated by the hard march,
and his strength exhausted by frequent attacks of illness.
Once he lay for eighty days in his hut, unable to proceed
further, harrowed by the wickedness about him which he
could not prevent, thinking about the sources of the Nile,
getting information from the natives, striving to do some
good among the people, and reading the Bible. He read it
through four times in about a year, while in the Manyuema
country. Little or no news from England arrived to cheer
him. Once he received a solitary letter; forty had been lost
on the way!

And now comes the crowning disappointment, which has
been well likened to that which Moses must have felt when
looking from Mt. Nebo upon the promised land he was not
permitted to enter. Dr. Livingstone had now come to the

Lualaba, which he hoped might be the Nile, although he feared it might be the Congo, as we now know it to be. A voyage down this river would settle the question. It would finish his task, and then at last he might go home; but here his
men mutinied and refused to go further. All his patience
and gentleness failed to have any effect upon them, and there
was nothing to do but to retrace his weary way in much
suffering and bodily weakness over five hundred miles to
Ujiji.

This journey was a most wretched one. Amid the wide
spread desolation caused by the slave-traders, it was impossible for Livingstone to make the natives understand that he
did not belong to the same set. Ambushes were set in the
forest for him and his company. Three times in one day did
Livingstone escape impending death. Twice spears were
thrown, once grazing his neck, the second time falling but
a foot away. A large tree to which fire had been applied for
the purpose of felling it, also came down within a yard of
him.

The one offset to the disappointment of returning to Ujiji,
was Dr. Livingstone's confident expectation that he should
there find fresh supplies, and the medicine he so much needed.
Arrived at last at Ujiji, "a mere ruckle of bones," as he himself says, he finds that once more his supplies have all been
plundered and sold. The wretch, Shereef, an Arab trader
to whom they had been consigned, had sold off the whole,
not leaving a single yard of calico out of 3000, or one string of
beads out of 700 pounds. He excused himself by saying that
he had divined on the Koran, and found out that Livingstone was dead, and therefore would need his goods no more.
The poor traveller had indeed fallen among thieves, and it
seemed as if there were none to come to his relief. But, never-
theless, help was coming to him even now.

CHAPTER XIII.

MEETING WITH STANLEY.

NOT many days after Livingstone's arrival at Ujiji, while he was still resting and striving to rally his strength and the splendid courage which even now was only staggered, not broken, Henry M. Stanley, who had been sent to look for him by Mr. J. G. Bennett of the *New York Herald*, appeared, "almost as an angel from heaven." This was on the tenth of November, 1871, by Stanley's reckoning, though somewhat earlier by Livingstone's. What comfort and refreshment did the lonely and disappointed explorer now find in the ample supplies, the bag of letters, the sight of a white face, and the welcome accents of his mother-tongue!

Neither Mr. Stanley nor Mr. Bennett had any personal interest in Dr. Livingstone. Mr. Bennett frankly admitted that it was only in the interests of his paper, and as a journalist, that he had sent out the expedition in search of the great missionary traveller. But Mr. Stanley, at least, soon felt that he had a personal regard toward his new-found friend. As for Livingstone, he kept saying: " You have brought me new life—you have brought me new life." So indeed it proved. Four meals a day of nourishing food, in contrast to his heretofore scanty and almost tasteless fare, brought back strength to his frame and flesh to his bones. But who can estimate the mental stimulus, the sense of companionship, that Stanley's coming brought him after his long and solitary wanderings in the wilderness?

Dr. Livingstone writes in his journal: "I felt in my destitution as if I were the man who went down from Jerusalem to Jericho, and fell among thieves; but I could not hope for Priest, Levite, or good Samaritan to come by on either side. . . . But when my spirits were at their lowest ebb, the good Samaritan was close at hand, for one morning Susi came running at the top of his speed, and gasped out, 'An Englishman! I see him!' and off he darted to meet him. The American flag at the head of a caravan told of the nationality of the stranger. Bales of goods, baths of tin, huge kettles, cooking pots, tents, etc., made me think, 'This man must be a luxurious trader, and not one at his wits' end like me.' It was Henry Moreland Stanley, the travelling correspondent of the *New York Herald*, sent by James Gordon Bennett, Jr., at an expense of more than £4,000, to obtain accurate information about Dr. Livingstone if living, and if dead to bring home my bones. The news he had to tell to one who had been two full years without any tidings from Europe made my whole frame thrill. The terrible fate that had befallen France — the telegraphic cables successfully laid in the Atlantic — the election of General Grant — the death of good Lord Clarendon, my constant friend — the proof that her Majesty's Government had not forgotten me in voting £1,000 for supplies, and many other points of interest, revived emotions that had lain dormant in Manyuema. Appetite returned, and instead of the spare, tasteless two meals a day, I ate four times daily, and in a week began to feel strong. I am not of a demonstrative turn — as cold indeed, as we islanders are usually reputed to be — but this disinterested kindness of Mr. Bennett, so nobly carried into effect by Mr. Stanley, was simply overwhelming."

Again he writes of Stanley: "He laid all he had at my service, divided his clothes into two heaps, and pressed one heap upon me; then his medicine chest; then his goods and everything he had, and to coax my appetite often cooked dainty dishes with his own hands."

Mr. Stanley remained with him during the winter, but when he returned in March, 1872, he earnestly besought Livingstone to go with him, urging that after sufficient recuperation in England he might return with renewed strength to take up the old problem again. Tempting as this proposal was—and no one could have blamed him for a moment had he accepted it—much as he must have yearned for country, friends and children, he steadfastly refused to leave the land until his work was finished. His thorough devotion to duty, his utter abandonment of self, were never more manifest than now. But a higher ambition than the finding out the true sources of the Nile urged him on. If his disclosures might but lead to the suppression of the east coast slave-trade, that, as he informed his friends, would be in his estimation a far greater feat than the discovery of all the sources together.

When at last the time came for the two companions to part, it was with the greatest reluctance that they tenderly bade each other farewell. Livingstone's appreciation of the service done him by Stanley was justly very great. He had proved a true friend to him, bringing him fresh strength and courage when almost at death's door, sharing all his comforts with him, and helping and cheering him in every way possible. It was Stanley on whom he now relied to send him trusty attendants; it was Stanley to whom he intrusted his journal and other documents. Stanley had been the only white man with whom he had talked for six years; more than that, during the four months that they had been together, Stanley had been his confidential friend.

And what did Stanley think of Livingstone? "God grant," he writes, "that if ever you take to travelling in Africa you will get as noble and true a man for your companion as David Livingstone! For four months and four days I lived with him in the same house, or in the same boat, or in the same tent, and I never found a fault in him. I am a man of a quick temper, and often without sufficient cause, I daresay, have broken the ties of friendship; but with Livingstone I never had cause for resentment, but each day's life with him added to my admiration for him."

CHAPTER XIV.

THE LAST JOURNEY.[1]

DR. LIVINGSTONE had accompanied his friend to Unyamyembe, where he was to wait until the latter should send him supplies and attendants from the coast. Here his stay was a somewhat dreary one. He had to wait much longer for his goods and men than he had anticipated, and there was so little to do that it was particularly trying for one of his intensely active temperament. Five days after Stanley's departure, occurred his fifty-ninth birthday, the entry for which day thus appears in his journal.

"March 19th, Birthday. My Jesus, my King, my life, my all; I again dedicate my whole self to Thee. Accept me, and grant, O gracious Father, that ere this year is gone I may finish my task. In Jesus' name I ask it. Amen, so let it be.—David Livingstone."

On the first of May he finished a letter to the *New York Herald*, trying to enlist American zeal to put a stop to the east coast slave-trade, and prayed for God's blessing to go with the effort. The concluding words of this letter were these: "All I can add in my loneliness, is, may Heaven's rich blessing come down on every one, American, English or Turk, who will help to heal the open sore of the world." It was felt that nothing could better represent the man than these words, which have been, consequently, inscribed on the tablet erected to his memory near his grave in Westminster Abbey. It was not noticed until some time after this selec-

6

tion had been made, that Livingstone wrote it exactly one year before his death, which occurred May 1st, 1873.

Sometimes amid the universal darkness and ignorance around him it is hard to believe that Africa shall ever be won to Christ, but he strengthens his own faith with such words as these, entered in his journal May 13th.

"He will keep His word—The gracious One, full of grace and truth—no doubt of it. He said, 'Him that cometh unto me I will in no wise cast out,' and 'Whatsoever ye shall ask in my name I will give it.' He WILL keep His word; then I can come and humbly present my petition, and it will be all right. Doubt is here inadmissible, surely.—David Livingstone."

Again, he writes of the way in which to gain the good will of the people, and thus secure a foundation for spiritual work among them. "June 21st. Nothing brings the Africans to place thorough confidence in Europeans, but a long course of well doing. . . . Goodness or unselfishness impresses their minds more than any kind of skill or power. They say, 'You have different hearts from ours; all black men's hearts are bad, but yours are good.' The prayer to Jesus for a new heart and right spirit at once commends itself as appropriate. Music has great influence on those who have musical ears, and often leads to conversion."

Then follow such pathetic entries as these: "July 3d. Wearisome waiting, this; and yet the men can not be here before the middle or end of next month. I have been sorely let and hindered in this journey, but it may have all been for the best. I will trust in Him to whom I commit my way.

"July 5th. Weary! weary!

"July 7th. Waiting wearily here, and hoping that the good and loving Father of all may favor me, and help me to finish my work quickly and well."

We also find from his journals that at this time Dr. Livingstone's mind was in a state of perpetual doubt and perplexity in regard to the Lualaba river, fearing that after all it might be the Congo. We are almost thankful that he never had his doubts solved, it would have been such a disappointment for him to have found for a certainty that this great river was *not* the Nile, even had he also known that henceforth it was to be known as the Livingstone river, and would perpetuate the memory of his life and labors for Africa.

In a letter to a friend he writes in reference to his endeavors to do all in his power towards suppressing the slave-trade: "To me it seems to be said, 'If thou forbear to deliver them that are drawn unto death, and those that are ready to be slain; if thou sayest, behold we knew it not, doth not He that pondereth the heart consider, and He that keepeth thy soul, doth He not know, and shall He not give to every one according to his works?' I have been led, unwittingly, into the slaving field of the Banians and Arabs in central Africa—I have seen the woes inflicted, and I must still work and do all I can to expose and mitigate the evils."

And again: "No one can estimate the amount of God-pleasing good that will be done, if by divine favor this awful slave-trade, into the midst of which I have come, be abolished. This will be something to have lived for, and the conviction has grown in my mind that it was *for this end* I have been detained so long."

His letters to the last show that his desire to discover

the sources of the Nile was only as a means of enabling him to open his mouth with power among men, and that the great desire of his heart was to arouse public feeling against the slave-trade, and to get that great hindrance to missionary effort and good of every kind forever swept away. Among the last words that he ever wrote were these: " I would forget all my cold, hunger, suffering and trials, if I could be the means of putting a stop to this cursed traffic."

At last Dr. Livingstone's escort arrived, among them Jacob Wainwright, who had been educated at the Nassick school, and who afterwards accompanied his master's body to England, and was one of the pall-bearers at the funeral in Westminster Abbey. To him we also owe the earliest narrative that appeared of the last eight months of Dr. Livingstone's life. This time Livingstone is not disappointed in his followers, whom he finds to be both faithful and capable.

It was in August that the party left Unyamyembe, proceeding towards Lakes Tanganyika and Bangweolo. Little of incident occurred on the first part of the march, but as the season advanced, the cold, rainy weather made their progress a perpetual struggle. It rained as if nothing but rain were ever known in the water-shed. The path lay across flooded rivers and long stretches of spongy marshland, and the inhabitants of the regions through which they passed often refused them food, and deceived them as to the way. Once a mass of furious ants attacked Livingstone by night, driving him from hut to hut in desperation.

Most constitutions would have succumbed after a few weeks of such exposure, and indeed, there is much sickness in the party. As for Livingstone, his sufferings are beyond all previous experience, but still he keeps on his way, and keeps his men together, showing an influence over them that is simply wonderful.

On his last birthday, March 19th, 1873, he makes the following entry in his journal: "Thanks to the Almighty Preserver of men for sparing me thus far on the journey of life! Can I hope for ultimate success? So many obstacles have arisen. Let not Satan prevail over me, oh! my good Lord Jesus."

And a few days later: "Nothing earthly will make me give up my work in despair. I encourage myself in the Lord my God and go forward".

But at last there is a limit to the endurance of even an "iron" constitution, although fortified as it was in Livingstone's case by an almost indomitable will, and his weakness at the beginning of April is pitiful. Still in spite of intense pain and bodily weakness he kept on his way, even when so exhausted that he had to be carried in a palanquin. The country was but a poor one at best, and was now flooded by heavy rains, so that even upon so called "dry land" the men often had to wade knee-deep in water as they carried their master onward.

On the 27th of April Dr. Livingstone wrote in his journal the last words he ever penned:

"Knocked up and remain—recover—sent to buy milch-goats. We are on the banks of the Molilamo."

Almost nothing could be found suited to the sick man's needs. Though suffering from intolerable thirst, water fit to drink was often unattainable, and the milch-goats were sought in vain; and so they pushed on for a day or two longer.

The word "recover" shows that Livingstone had no anticipation of immediate death. It has been observed that

such cases of malarial poisoning are usually unattended with
such expectation, or with such messages to friends and
expressions of faith as would be natural to Christian men, did
they realize the near approach of death. But where one is
ready to go, it matters little how suddenly the messenger
calls him hence.

April 29th was the last day of the great explorer's travels
upon earth, and then he had to be lifted from his hut to the
palanquin. At last they reached Chitambo's village in Ilala,
where he had to lie under the eaves of a house in a drizzling
rain till a hut could be prepared for him. Then he was laid
on a rude bed in the hut for the night. The next day he
lay quietly all day, the attendants knowing that death was
not far off. During the early part of the night following,
nothing occurred to attract attention, but about four in the
morning the boy who lay at his door keeping watch called
in alarm for Susi, one of his old servants, fearing that their
master was dead. By the light of the candle still burning,
they saw him kneeling by his bedside as if in the act of
prayer, his head buried in his hands on the pillow. Praying
as he went, he had gone on his last journey, and without a
single attendant. Alone, yet not alone, for He who had sus-
tained him through so many trials and dangers had gone
with him through the " swelling of Jordan," and brought
him safe to the celestial country.

CHAPTER XV.

THE LAST RESTING-PLACE.

DURING all the trying experiences of this last exploration, Dr. Livingstone had been cheered by the special devotion of two of the attendants, Susi and Chumah, who had been with him long and loved him well. Their tenderness to him had been like that of a mother to a dying child, and now that their master was gone, their fidelity still showed itself in the determination that every effort should be made to convey his body to Zanzibar. Surely, if anything were needed to commend the African race to our sympathy and respect, the loyalty, affection and courage now shown by all Livingstone's followers might well have this effect. Although it involved nine months of hard and perilous travel, their resolve was carried out without faltering. The ordinary risks of such a journey were by no means small, but the superstitious horror of death everywhere prevalent now made it dangerous in the extreme. They endeavored to keep Chitambo, the chief of the village where Livingstone died, in ignorance of his death, fearing lest a ruinous fine should be inflicted upon them. The secret, however, oozed out, but fortunately the chief was reasonable in his demands.

Susi and Chumah now became the leaders of the company, and nobly did they fulfil their task. They first made a careful inventory of Dr. Livingstone's personal effects, then deposited all his papers and scientific instruments in

water-tight boxes, so that they would not be injured in ford-
ing rivers.   Though the later entries in his journal had been
made only with the juice of plants upon old London newspapers, they too, were carefully preserved, so that everything
reached England in perfect safety.

Jacob Wainwright was asked to read the English burial
service, which he did in the presence of all.   Then arrangements were made for drying and embalming the body, the
heart and other internal organs first having been removed
and buried.   After having been dried in the sun for fourteen
days, during which time the men took turns in keeping
watch night and day, the body was wrapped in cloth, the
legs bent inward at the knees, and the whole enclosed in a
large piece of bark in the shape of a cylinder.   Over this
again a piece of sail cloth was sewed, and the package was
lashed to a pole so as to be carried by two men.   Jacob
Wainwright carved the inscription on the tree where the
body had rested and under which the heart was buried, and
Chitambo was charged to keep the grass cleared away, and
to protect the rude monument, consisting of two posts and a
cross-piece, which they had erected.

They then set out on their homeward journey, which was
made more serious still by the frequent ravages of sickness.
The tribes through which they passed were as a general
thing friendly to them, but not always.   On one occasion
there was a regular fight, and at another village the inhabitants showed so much opposition, that it was resolved to
pack the remains so as to look exactly like a bale of mer-
chandise.   This having been done, a bundle of mapira stalks,
cut into lengths of about six feet, was then enveloped in
cloth, so as to imitate a dead body about to be buried.
This was sent back along the way they had already tra-

versed, as if they had changed their minds and had concluded to bury the body. As it grew dark the bearers began to throw away the stalks and wrappings, and when all were disposed of they returned to their companions. The villagers' suspicions having been thus allayed, they were suffered to go on unmolested.

The party reached Bagamoio with their precious burden in February, 1874. Soon after Dr. Livingstone's remains were placed on a cruiser bound for Zanzibar, and from thence sent on to England, reaching Southampton on the 15th of April.

The latest intelligence that we have had in regard to the devoted Susi, is that found in a paper of March, 1887, and is very cheering to hear. • He had then been recently baptized by a member of the Universities' Mission, receiving the new name of David, in memory of the noble man who had first taught him what it was to be a Christian.

To many it seemed so incredible that the real body of Livingstone should have been brought all the distance from the heart of Africa to England, that some positive means of identification was necessary to put their doubts at rest. This was supplied by the false joint in the arm that the lion had crushed. High medical authorities who had examined the fractured arm years before, certified that there could not be a doubt as to these being the remains of "one of the greatest men of the human race — David Livingstone."

On the 18th of April, 1874, the remains of the great missionary traveler were committed to their last resting place in Westminster Abbey, where crowds of people listened to the impressive funeral services, and joined in the simple but touching words of the hymn:

O God of Bethel, by whose hand
Thy people still are fed ;
Who through this weary pilgrimage
Hast all our fathers led !

. . . .

" Oh spread thy covering wings around,
Till all our wanderings cease,
And at our Father's loved abode,
Our souls arrive in peace."

Many of Livingstone's friends had come to pay their last tribute of respect and love; some who had helped to lay " Ma Robert" in her lonely grave twelve years before ; one who had found the long lost missionary, and brought him back to life and hope; one who had himself first read the triumphant words of the burial service over the mortal remains of his loved and trusted master.   All these now helped to bear him to his last resting place.   And one more was there, the aged father of his beloved Mary, the one who had been the means under God of bringing him to his life work in Africa.   Sorrowfully they laid him to rest, and yet with rejoicing, for they knew that the good and faithful servant had entered into the joy of his Lord.

"Open the Abbey doors and bear him in
To sleep with king and statesman, chief and sage,
The missionary come of weaver kin,
But great by work that brooks no lower wage.

" He needs no epitaph to guard a name
Which men shall prize while worthy work is known ;
He lived and died for good — be that his fame ;
Let marble crumble ; this is Living—stone."

CHAPTER XVI.

ESTIMATE OF HIS LIFE-WORK.

"GOD has taken away the greatest man of his genera-
tion, for Dr. Livingstone stood alone." So wrote
Florence Nightingale to his sorrowing daughter, and no
careful reader of his life can fail to recognize in him one
of the grandest heroes not merely of this, but of any age.

As a missionary explorer he stood alone, travelling
29,000 miles in Africa, adding to the known portion of the
globe about a million square miles, discovering lakes N'gami,
Shirwa, Nyassa, Moero and Bangweolo, the upper Zambesi
and many other rivers, and the wonderful Victoria Falls.
He was also the first European to traverse the entire length
of Lake Tanganyika, and to travel over the vast water-shed
near Lake Bangweolo, and, through no fault of his own, he
only just missed the information that would have set at rest
his conjectures as to the Nile sources. He greatly increased
the knowledge of the geography, fauna and flora of the
interior, yet never lost sight of the great objects of his life,
the putting down of the slave-trade, and the evangelization
of Africa.

His attainments as a physician were of no mean order.
The London Lancet, expressing the hearty appreciation of
the medical profession, says: " Few men have disappeared
from our ranks more universally deplored, as few have
served in them with a higher purpose, or shed upon them
the lustre of a purer devotion."

During the thirty-three years of Dr. Livingstone's service for Africa, his labors as a philanthropist and a missionary were unceasing. Largely as a result of these labors, that infamous slave-trade, against which he struck the first blow, has now been obliterated along thousands of miles of African coast where once it held full sway, and all Christian nations have banded together to forbid and punish this traffic throughout a vast area in the interior, planting stations for 1,500 miles inland for the enforcement of the law.

As a missionary his immediate success may not have appeared great; he was but a forerunner "preparing the way of the Lord." His was the work of the pioneer, blazing the way, making the rough places smooth for others to follow, opening the country for Christianity to enter in. But scarcely had the civilized world learned of his death, before, inspired by his example, there began a mighty movement on behalf of Africa. The first fruits of that last dying prayer for the country to which he had given his life were seen in the establishment near Lake Nyassa of a mission founded by the churches of Scotland, henceforth to be known by the name of Livingstonia. As soon as Stanley knew that his friend was no more, he resolved to carry on his efforts in opening up Africa to civilization. A thousand days' journey brought him from Zanzibar to the mouth of the Congo, the news of which reaching England, the next vessel that sailed for the "dark continent" carried missionaries to help enlighten its darkness. Wherever he has gone Stanley's explorations have left behind them a line of Christian light. Robert Arthington now pours out his fortune, giving in ten years over two millions of dollars. Missionaries hasten to the interior. All denominations vie with each other in Christian zeal. King Leopold, of Belgium, resolves to "live for Africa." The fruit of this resolve is seen in the Congo Free State.

The statement has been made, and it scarcely seems exaggerated, that there is probably no mission field in the world that is at present attracting the attention of the church at large as much as that of Africa. All eyes turn with interest, especially to that wonderful Congo Free State, with its rich and vast area, and its population of fifty millions of inhabitants, with its express promises of government protection and favor to all religious undertakings, and its guarantee to the natives of freedom of conscience and religious toleration. True, with all that is encouraging in its outlook, the new liquor traffic is threatening its peace and prosperity, but already the abhorrence of Christendom regarding this death-dealing traffic is making itself felt, and we can but believe that this monstrous iniquity will be throttled while it is yet in its infancy.

All through that region of eastern and central Africa in which Livingstone spent so many years, and for which he uttered so many prayers, new mission stations are being planted, the Universities' Mission, the London Missionary Society, the Free and Established churches of Scotland, the Methodists, Swiss, and other societies all having representatives there. So great an expansion of missionary enterprise could never have taken place in so short a time but for Dr. Livingstone's energy in opening Africa, and for his enthusiasm in enlisting recruits for his loved field.

At a moderate estimate there are now between thirty and forty missionary societies working in Africa, and over 500 missionaries spreading the glad tidings of salvation. The converts, though already numbering many tens of thousands, are as yet but a handful among the two hundred millions with which Africa teems, but their number is steadily growing, and when we remember that until a few years ago nothing was known of the vast interior, we have reason to thank God and take courage. Soon the continent will be crossed by a network of railways, penetrated by explorers, settled by traders, and dotted over with Christian missions. Already roads are being built and railways constructed, steamboats sail up and down the great lakes and rivers, and a submarine cable has been laid. It will not be long ere all these millions of inhabitants will be practically within the reach of Christian missionaries.

Was Dr. Livingstone's life then a failure? Was it a wasted service, that ended only in defeat as he breathed his last in that lonely hut in Ilala? These few years that have elapsed since his death have already seen realized the deepest desires of his heart. Africa is open, the slave-trade is condemned, a wonderful impetus has been given to the planting of Christian missions, and—the end is not yet.

CHAPTER XVII.

LIVINGSTONE AS A MAN.

BUT beyond and above Doctor Livingstone's greatness as a missionary, a physician, a philanthropist, and an explorer, it is the character of the man that shines out pre-eminently great. The rare symmetry of this was such that one who knew him bears witness that he was the most Christ-like man he ever knew. Another says that she never knew any one who gave to her more the idea of power over other men, such power as Christ showed while on earth, the power of love and purity combined.

A friend of his earlier days remarks: "There was truly an indescribable charm about him, which, with all his rather ungainly ways and by no means winning face, attracted almost every one, and which helped him so much in his after-wanderings in Africa. He won those who came near him by a kind of spell."

This power lay first of all in his large-heartedness, his genuine kindliness and consideration for others, which prompted him to be just as courteous, just as *Christian* let us rather say, in his treatment of the poor, ignorant black as in that of the most polished and learned European. Few men have the ability that he possessed of taking an "all around" view of things; he could look at matters not merely from a narrow standpoint of his own, but from the standpoint of others also; he needed far less than most of us, the injunction, "put yourself in his place."

"When a chief has made any inquiries of us," he observes,

"we have found that we gave most satisfaction in our answers when we tried to fancy ourselves in the position of the interrogator, and him that of a poor uneducated fellow-countryman in England. The polite, respectful way of speaking, and behavior of what we call 'a thorough gentleman' almost always secures the friendship and good will of the Africans."

And again he writes to the same effect: "Whether we approach the downtrodden victims of the slave-trade in sultry Africa, or our poor brethren in the streets who have neither warmth, shelter, nor home, we must employ the same agency to secure their confidence — the magic power of kindness; a charm which may be said to be one of the discoveries of modern days. This charm may not act at once, nor may its effects always be permanent, but the feelings which the severity of their lot has withered will in time spring up like the tender grass after rain."

One secret of his success in winning the friendship of the natives lay in the fact that his kindness to them was marred by no spirit of condescension, and that he thoroughly recognized their manhood. In the rudest black, as well as in the most cultivated white man, he saw a brother man, made in the image of God, and therefore to be treated with courtesy and respect.

Doctor Livingstone's tact and consideration for the feelings of others are strikingly shown in his treatment of the native doctors. The following extract is taken from his first book of travels: "Those doctors who have inherited their profession as an heir-loom generally possess some valuable knowledge, the result of long observation. The rest are usually quacks. With the regular practitioners I always remained on the best terms, and refrained from appearing to doubt their skill in the presence of their patients. Any explanation in private was thankfully received, and wrong treatment readily changed for more rational methods. English drugs were eagerly accepted; and we always found medical knowledge an important aid in convincing the people that we were anxious for their welfare. The surgical skill of the natives is at a low ebb. No one ever attempted to remove a tumor except by external application. A man had one on the nape of his neck as large as a child's head. Some famous doctor attempted to dissolve it by kindling on it a little fire, made of a few small pieces of medicinal roots. I removed this tumor, as I did an immense number of others, with perfect safety," but "I refrained from attending the sick unless their own doctors wished it, or had given up the case. This prevented all offense to the native practitioners, and limited my services, as I desired, to the severer attacks."

Dr. Livingstone showed the same spirit as was in his Master in taking a genuine interest in those about him. Nothing was too trivial for him to be interested in if it concerned his brother-man. One or two extracts from his journals will suffice here. "As we were sleeping one night outside a hut, but near enough to hear what was going on within, an anxious mother began to grind her corn about two o'clock in the morning. 'Ma,' inquired a little girl, 'why grind in the dark?' Mamma advised sleep, and administered material for a sweet dream to her darling. 'I grind meal to buy a cloth from the strangers which will make you look a little lady.' An observer of these primitive races is struck continually with such little trivial touches of genuine human nature."

Truly "one touch of nature makes the whole world kin."

7

"It is rather a minute thing to mention, and it will only be understood by those who have children of their own, but the cries of the little ones in their infant sorrows are the same in tone, at different ages, here as all over the world. We have been perpetually reminded of home and family by the wailings which were once familiar to parental ears and heart, and felt thankful that to the sorrows of childhood our children would never have superadded the heart-rending woes of the slave-trade."

Dr. Livingstone's wonderful patience has already been spoken of. Under the most trying circumstances he still preserved his self-control. Occasionally, as in the case of the Boers' unprovoked assault on Kolobeng and Limaue, he could find no excuse for those in fault, but generally he was quick to see extenuating circumstances. For instance, after being deserted by some of his men he says: " I have taken all the runaways back again ; after trying the independent life, they will behave better. Much of their ill conduct may be ascribed to seeing that after the flight of the Johanna men I was entirely dependent on them. More enlightened people often take advantage of men in similar circumstances; though I have seen pure Africans come out generously to aid one abandoned to their care. I have faults myself."

In another place he speaks of sometimes being ashamed when he finds that he has been vexed at the natives without cause. Of course they are often stupid, but perhaps no more so than servants at home often are, and the conduct of white men must frequently appear to them silly or half-insane.

Another marked trait in Livingstone was his capacity for solitude, enabling him to endure an amount of loneliness that would have crushed any ordinary man. For, notwithstanding his interest in and love for the natives, he must often have felt an inexpressible desire for the companionship of those who could understand his motives and who by birth and education were fitted to be his intimate associates. His keen love of nature, his close habits of observation, must have helped him to pass cheerfully through his many lonely hours; but, best of all, he had constantly with him the presence of Him who had said, "I will never leave thee nor forsake thee." The weary, tread-mill-like march he says was particularly favorable to meditation, and many must have been the hours of sweet communion held with his Master.

Dr. Livingstone's courage in exposing himself to danger if in the path of duty is no less to be commented on, though he himself never speaks of it. Dr. Moffat gives several instances as samples of what was habitual to him, only one of which we cite. Once, he tells us, when Dr. Livingstone was engaged in his special mission-work, a messenger came in the greatest haste to solicit his attendance on a native who had been attacked in a wood by a rhinoceros, and frightfully wounded. Livingstone's friends urged him not to take the risk of riding through the woods at night, exposed to the rhinoceros and other harmful beasts as he was certain to be, telling him that it was sure death to venture; but he felt that it was only a Christian duty to save the poor fellow's life if possible, and resolved to go in spite of the danger to himself. Starting at once to relieve the sufferer he forced his way for ten miles, in midnight darkness, through tangled brake and thicket, till he reached the spot where the wounded man lay, only to find him dead But was it a wasted sacrifice? Was it not rather as the sweet ointment spilled out of love to the Lord?

, Although the recipient of prizes, degrees, gold medals

and honors of many kinds, Dr. Livingstone still preserved
an unusually childlike, humble spirit. Once when a great
man expressed admiration for his wonderful achievements,
he replied: "They are not wonderful; it was only what any
one else could do that had the will." Ah! but was not such
a *will* wonderful?   What too shall we say of such modesty
as this? "Men may think I covet fame, but I make it a
rule never to read aught written in my praise."

One who had known him as a student with Mr. Cecil
writes: "I might sum up my impression of him in two
words — Simplicity and Resolution. Now, after nearly
forty years, I remember his step, the characteristic forward
tread, firm, simple, resolute, neither fast nor slow, no hurry
and no dawdle, but which evidently meant — getting there.'
Simple and resolute Dr. Livingstone was to the last. With
childlike trustfulness, combined with equal fearlessness, he
was able to disarm the fierceness of savage men, where the
least appearance of timidity might have been fatal.

His tremendous force of will carried him through dangers and obstacles before which a weaker nature would have
quickly succumbed. Once having made up his mind that
a certain course was the path of duty, nothing could cause
him to swerve from it. This will-power availed not only for
himself, but for his followers also, instilling courage and
devotion to duty into the minds of those who heretofore
had been weak and irresolute.

Livingstone's faithfulness to promises has already been
dwelt upon. Whether made to the Geographical Society,
or to the poor, helpless, ignorant African, it mattered not.
Once made, a promise was faithfully carried out.

The description of the ideal missionary leader, as given
in one of his own books, is so striking a picture of his own

character that we cannot forbear quoting it : "The qualities required in a missionary leader are not of the common kind. He ought to have physical and moral courage of the highest order, and a considerable amount of cultivation and energy, balanced by patient determination ; and above all these are necessary a calm, Christian zeal, and anxiety for the main spiritual results of the work." Yet this characterization does not necessarily give one the idea of such meekness and love as, in addition, belonged to our hero. It was the blending together of all these qualities that made the so nearly perfect man.

Do we seem to exaggerate? As Professor Blaikie says in his *Life of Livingstone*, while often eulogiums on the dead conceal one half of the truth, and fill the eye with the other half, here there is really nothing to conceal. A plain, honest statement of the truth regarding him is Livingstone's highest praise.

Mr. Stanley has written very fully of the impression that Dr. Livingstone made upon him. Let us listen to him once more as he goes still further into details :

"I grant he is not an angel; but he approaches to that being as near as the nature of a living man will allow. His gentleness never forsakes him ; his hopefulness never deserts him. No harassing anxieties, distraction of mind, long separation from home and kindred, can make him complain. He thinks 'all will come out right at last;' he has such faith in the goodness of Providence. . . .

"Another thing that specially attracted my attention was his wonderfully retentive memory. If we remember the many years he has spent in Africa, deprived of books, we may well think it an uncommon memory that can recite whole poems from Burns, Tennyson, Longfellow, Whittier, and Lowell. . . .

"His religion is not of the theoretical kind, but it is a constant, earnest, sincere practice. . . . In him religion exhibits its loveliest features: it governs his conduct, not only toward his servants, but toward the natives, the bigoted Mohammedans, and all who come in contact with him. Without it, Livingstone, with his ardent temperament, his enthusiasm, his high spirit and courage, must have become uncompanionable, and a hard master. Religion has tamed him, and made him a Christian gentleman; the crude and wilful have been refined and subdued; religion has made him the most companionable of men and indulgent of masters,— a man whose society is pleasurable to a degree. From being thwarted and hated in every possible way by the Arabs and half-castes, upon his first arrival at Ujiji, he has, through his uniform kindness and mild, pleasant temper, won all hearts. I observed that universal respect was paid to him. Even the Mohammedans never passed his house without calling to pay their compliments, and to say, ' The blessing of God rest on you!' . . .
Each Sunday morning he gathers his little flock around him, and reads prayers, and a chapter from the Bible, in a natural, unaffected, and sincere tone; and afterwards delivers a short address in the Kisawahili language, about the subject read to them, which is listened to with evident interest and attention."

The latest words that we have seen from Stanley, testifying at once to the native nobility of the African, and to the personal influence which Livingstone exerted over himself, are to this effect: "I have been in Africa for seventeen years, and I have never met a man who would kill me if I folded my hands. What I wanted and what I have been endeavoring to ask for the poor Africans has been the

good offices of Christians, ever since Livingstone taught
me during those four months that I was with him. In 1871
I went to him as prejudiced as the biggest atheist in London.
I was out there away from a worldly world. I saw this
solitary old man there, and asked myself, 'Why on earth
does he stop here?' For months after we met, I found
myself listening to him, and wondering at the old man's carrying out all that was said in the Bible. Little by little his
sympathy for others became contagious; mine was awakened;
seeing his piety, his gentleness, his zeal, his earnestness, and
how he went quietly about his business, I was converted by
him, although he had not tried to do it. How sad that the
good old man died so soon! how joyful he would have been
if he could have seen what has since happened there!"

A few years ago a missionary travelling in the Rovuma
country met a native with the relic of an old coat, evidently
of English manufacture, over his right shoulder. It seemed
from the man's statement, that ten years before he had travelled some little distance with a white man who had given
him the coat. A man whom to have once seen and talked
to was to remember for life; a white man who treated black
men as his brothers, and whose memory would always be
cherished all through the Rovuma Valley; a man, short of
stature, with bushy mustache and keen, piercing eye, whose
words and manner were always kind and gentle; a man
whom as a leader all men were glad to follow; a man who
knew the way to the hearts of all.

Many and brilliant have been the eulogiums in which
the learned and the great have vied with each other to do
honor to the name of the great explorer; but among them
all none touches the heart more deeply than the simple
tribute of this untutored savage. Like the touching fidelity

of the black body-guard who bore his remains safely to the sea, it is an earnest and a prophecy of the reverent gratitude with which in all coming time the millions of that "dark continent," to whose redemption his life was given, will cherish the memory of the hero and apostle of Africa, — David Livingstone.

NOTE.—The material for this sketch has been mainly drawn from Prof. Blaikie's "Personal Life of David Livingstone," and from Livingstone's three books, "Missionary Travels in South Africa," "The Zambesi and its Tributaries," and the "Last Journals." Some information has also been derived from missionary periodicals. Liberal quotation has been made from Dr. Livingstone's letters and journals, in the belief that his own words would best represent the man.

CPSIA information can be obtained
at www.ICGtesting.com
Printed in the USA
LVHW101347150419
614218LV00006B/13/P